SPIRITUAL WARFARE

AND THE

BELIEVER

I0155367

McDougal & Associates

Servants of Christ and Stewards of the
Mysteries of God

Endorsements

Dr. Fluitt came to South Africa to a remote village called Maphophe in Limpopo Province. He preached here for two weeks about "The Authority of the Believer" and "Spiritual Warfare." He showed us what it means to be a Christian and the power vested in us through the name of Jesus, the Holy Spirit, and the blood of Jesus. Dr. Mike symbolized a Christian believer's life as an ambassador who carries the weight of his country in a foreign land. He showed us that an ambassador, even though he eats food and drinks water from the foreign land, does not belong there. If someone touches him, they are touching his country as well.

He showed us the power vested in a traffic officer, outlining that the mere gesture of the hand of a traffic officer must be obeyed because his hand has the authority of the president of the country. If he is disobeyed, the person who disobeyed him is offending the whole country.

Likewise, a Christian believer carries the heavenly authority of creating, commanding, and enforcing obedience over the enemy. When we believe what the Word of God says, the Bible teaches us that we can do the same miracles Jesus did. These messages taught us to know that we have authority over all forces in the world.

Our village and the surrounding villages are made up of people who believe in superstition, witchcraft, and ancestral worship. These people are very afraid of evil spirits. Even the church has been afraid of these spirits. This was all regarded as part of our culture and traditions, but it brought poverty on the land. People who had money were afraid to use it in fear of being bewitched.

After Dr. Mike's teachings on the power and authority of believers that we have in Jesus Christ and "Spiritual Warfare," we started to hear testimonies of people being freed from witchcraft and demonic possession. Christians started to realize that the One in them is greater than the one in the world, and the church started to prosper financially.

The membership of the church has now risen to about five hundred from the less than eighty people we had before, and Dr. Mike came in 2009 to ordain eight new ministers to help with ministering to the many people now in the church. We have now purchased a new tract of land and are building a new church building to accommodate two thousand, plus all of the new people coming to Maphophe to see what God is doing here.

Through the teachings Dr. Fluitt gave us, we see a great change in our church and in the entire society. People are now more concerned about believing God's Word than any written material that brings prosperity to the church. Among the church members, people are getting jobs, buying cars, and building houses. Our church services are very different than before, and we experience miracles every day. Thank you, Dr. Mike, for visiting our area and for preaching God's Word about the power of believers. You have awakened the power we now use every day. May God bless you!

Simon Shirinda,
Senior Pastor,
Born Again Christian Church,
Maphophe, Limpopo Province,
Republic of South Africa

❄

To God be the glory, in 2007 I took a class being taught by Dr. Fluitt on "The Authority of the Believer and Spiritual Warfare." I count it a blessing to be one of the many graduates of Dr. Mike Fluitt's dynamic, powerful, and anointed teachings.

I took the class as an intercessor. I would pray for people in the name of Jesus, and they would be healed. You could see that they were doing well for a season, and then they would go back into their sin and be sick again. I thought something I was doing wrong in my life was causing this.

Through taking this class, I realized that the strongman was not being bound. I came to realize that the "generals" had to be bound, and the blood of Jesus applied, and the fruits of and gifts of the Holy Spirit must be loosed in our lives. When I began to do this, curses began to be broken off of my life and those of other people, and we were being completely healed. Jesus died for us to have authority over the enemy in our life and every believer's life. Because of this, my life will never be the same, and now my prayer life has the power of Jesus in operation.

Pastor Zelma Moore,
Associate Pastor, Zion Hill Family Church
Pineville, Louisiana

❄

"The Authority of the Believer" and "Spiritual Warfare" … these classes have been a blessing to me and my family, friends, and church family. Studying these subjects has enlightened my future and opened up the understanding of my past. I encourage you and your loved ones to read this book, for it will literally change your life. Your life will never be the same again. TO GOD BE THE GLORY!

Minister Fannie Reed
Zion Hill Family Church
Pineville, Louisiana

SPIRITUAL WARFARE
AND THE
BELIEVER

BY

DR. MICHAEL FLUITT

Spiritual Warfare and the Believer
Copyright © 2023—Michael Fluitt
ALL RIGHTS RESERVED

Unless otherwise noted, all Scripture references are from the *Holy Bible, New King James Version*, copyright © 1979, 1980, 1982, 1990 by Thomas Nelson, Inc., Nashville, Tennessee. References marked NLT are from *The New Living Translation of the Bible*, copyright © 1996 by Tyndale House Publishers, Inc., Wheaton, Illinois. References marked NIV are from the *New International Version of the Bible*, copyright © 1973, 1978, 1984 by Biblica, Colorado Springs, Colorado. References marked KJV are from *The Holy Bible, King James Version*, Public domain. All rights reserved. Used by permission.

Cover art by Kimberly Fluitt Zachary

Published by:

McDougal & Associates
18896 Greenwell Springs Road
Greenwell Springs, LA 70739
www.ThePublishedWord.com

McDougal & Associates is dedicated to spreading the Gospel of the Lord Jesus Christ to as many people as possible in the shortest time possible.

ISBN: 978-1-950398-88-1

Printed on demand in the U.S., the U.K., Australia, and the UAE
For Worldwide Distribution

Dedication

This book is dedicated to the glory of:

God the Father,
God the Son, and
God the Holy Spirit,

Without Whom this book
could not have been possible,
Without Whom we have no
power over the enemy.

Acknowledgments

For the front cover design:

Kimberly Fluitt Zachary

For editing of the material:

Janice Fluitt
Tommy J. Bowers
and
Harold McDougal

Contents

FOREWORD BY JANICE FLUITT

As of this writing, Mike and I have been married for fifty-six years. Unfortunately, God was not the center of our marriage for the first ten years, and Satan had a field day. After Mike came back to the Lord, he attended Bible college and came away with the reality that he had (and we have) authority over the enemy in our lives. He did further research and studies and began to teach on "The Authority of the Believer" and "Spiritual Warfare." Today, many years later, these are still two of his favorite subjects to share with others: the authority that believers have over Satan and how to use that authority against him.

It is so rewarding to see others taking their rightful place in the Kingdom of God. Their lives and the lives of others around them begin to change as they take authority over the enemies in their lives.

When we went to South Africa, we were privileged to sit with a true king. He shared with us what could be expected growing up as the child of a king. He also spoke of the power his words had in his father's kingdom. Our eyes were opened to the reality and insight of the authority we have as a child of THE KING of KINGS. We live so far below what God intends for us to have.

The devil, many times, takes control of our lives, and sadly, we let him. It is time to take our rightful place as a child of the KING of KINGS with authority and to tell the devil to back off. This book will enlighten you by giving you the knowledge of how to deal with the devil and the authority you have over him and his cohorts. It will also teach you the authority you have as a child of the King and how to take your rightful place. When you receive this powerful insight into your heart, no demon in Hell will be able to stand against you.

Enjoy reading this book and expect to come away with the knowledge of how to attain victory over Satan and his cohorts that come against your life.

Rev. Janice K. Fluitt, RN
Co-Founder, Africa Ministries

INTRODUCTION

In this book, we will introduce you, the reader, to the concept of deliverance of the human, spirit, soul, and body, evicting unclean spirits from Satan from their human home. THIS IS NOT SOMETHING TO BE PLAYED WITH. IT IS NO JOKE OR GAME, BUT IS REAL AND, AT TIMES, VERY DANGEROUS. If you are not submitted to the Lord Jesus Christ and His Word and filled with His Holy Spirit, then DO NOT attempt to do the things outlined in this book.

In this, my second book, there are twelve teachings and twelve chapters. We will look at the twelve generals, or "strongmen," of Satan. Remember, in the book, *The Authority of the Believer*, I wrote of the book by Mary K. Baxter, *A Divine Revelation of Hell*,[1] and there she said that there is a ranking order among the demon spirits, just as there is a rank in the heavenly angels and our earthly armies. We will look at these spirits and identify them and their roll

1. New Kensington, PA (Whitaker House: 1997)

in the destruction of God's creation, as well as their influence on all mankind.

As we identify these "generals" or "strongmen," you will begin to see their roll in the dark underworld that Satan controls. We will see the misery they are inflicting on the men and women of this earth. Why? Because so many don't believe (or understand) that they have the authority, or, as defined in *Webster's Dictionary*, "delegated power, the right to command, to enforce obedience, and to make final decisions" over the works of the devil in their lives, those of their family and their church, and to cast them out. Nor do they know how to identify these demonic spirits. Let's look, once again, at a quote from Baxter's book.

The book describes what Baxter saw in the Spirit during the forty nights that Jesus visited her. For thirty of those nights He took her into Hell to show her who and what was there and what it was like. On pages 38, 39 and 40, she described what she saw and heard:

We went on together. I followed closely behind Him crying. For many days I had been crying, and I could not shake off the very presence of Hell which was ever before me. I cried mostly inside. My spirit was very sad.

16

We arrived at the right leg of Hell. Looking ahead, I saw that we were on a pathway which was dry and burned. Screams filled the dirty air, and the stench of death was everywhere. The odor was sometimes so repugnant that it made me sick to my stomach. Everywhere was darkness except for the light which emanated from the pits, which dotted the landscape as far as I could see.

All at once, demons of all kinds were going past us. Imps growled at us as they went by. Demon spirits of all sizes and shapes were talking to each other. Out ahead of us, a big demon was giving orders to small ones. We stopped to listen, and Jesus said, "There is also an invisible army of evil forces that we do not see here—demons such as evil spirits of sickness."

"Go!" the larger demon said to the smaller imps and devils. "Do many evil things. Break up homes and destroy families. Seduce the weak Christians, and misinstruct and mislead as many as you can. You shall have your reward when you return. "Remember, you must be careful of those who have genuinely accepted Jesus as their Savior. They have the power to cast you out" (see Mark 16:17-18).

Everywhere I looked were demons and devils. The biggest of these demons, I learned from the Lord, were getting their orders straight from Satan.

These "bigger demons" that Mary K. Baxter spoke of are the generals or "strongmen" that we will be looking at in the following pages.

I have taught both of these teachings, which have been become books, for many years. There are audio CDs also available for these teachings for a fee and for the asking. The entire outline is available online by going to mdfluitt@hotmail. com and requesting the outline. I have now taught this for over twenty-five years in many churches in America. It was initially taught to ministers only, until 2007, when the Holy Spirit said to me, "Take it to the Church." It has now been taught in many churches in South Africa, Malawi, Zimbabwe, and Mozambique. Copies have also gone out to Nigeria, Uganda, Angola, Australia, and Pakistan, and to many Christians in churches across America.

As you read and study the information given in this book, I pray that it will enlighten you in the realm of the spirits and open your eyes to the things God has in store for those who love Him and are obedient to His Word. This material represents many hours and years of prayer, study, and practical application in the areas of teaching, counseling, and deliverance. May God RICHLY bless you in your study of the Word and in the reading of this book, and may it set you and your family free.

Dr. Michael D. Fluitt
Email: mdfluitt@hotmail.com

TO MICHAEL FROM JESUS

Michael, it is your assignment to teach the Body of Christ who they are and what they are in Me. Teach them that the devil, not them, is the one who has been defeated by Me. It was from him that I took the keys of Hell, death, and the grave and rose victorious with ALL power and authority both in Heaven and Earth. Teach them that it was My power and authority that I transferred to them for the purpose of staying victorious over ALL of the works of the devil. Teach them that he was, and still is, defeated and subject to My name, Jesus, and that they have My permission to use My name against him any time, any place, and to expect victory when they do.

CHAPTER 1

SPIRIT OF DIVINATION

DEFINITION: *"To determine, by lot or magical scroll, witchcraft, tarot cards, tea leaves, etc., the future."*

In my first book, we have looked at the authority of the believer from a biblical prospective and studied The Source of Our Authority, the Power Behind the Authority, the Confidence We Can Have in Knowing that We Have This Authority, Using This Authority Over the Works of the Enemy, the Divine Protection and Immunity We Can Walk in with This Authority, and finally, The Authority to Lay Hands on the Sick, Oppressed, and Possessed and See Them Healed, Delivered, and Set Free from the Influences of the Enemy. All of this is needed as we minister in the Spirit to individuals who need healing.

The primary thing, first of all, is to determine the salvation status of the person you are about to minister deliverance to. If they are a Christian, then proceed with the deliverance. If they are not a Christian, then lead them in the sinner's prayer, asking God to forgive them of their sins and asking Jesus to come into their lives as their Lord and Savior. We will see the importance of this later in the book.

THE SPIRIT OF DIVINATION IS SATAN'S FIRST GENERAL

NOTE: The works of the flesh cannot be bound. They are free-will acts of the individual person, but they are controlled by demonic spirits that can and must be bound in order to set the person free. Galatians 5:19-21 lists the works of the flesh that we see in the life of those who are in need of healing or deliverance.

This word *manifestation* literally means "the demonstration of the existence, reality, or presence of a person, object, or quality: a manifestation of ill will, one of the forms in which someone or something, such as an individual, a divine or demonic being, or idea is revealed." In other words, we can see on the outside of the person what is happening on the inside by what they are doing or exhibiting in the natural or flesh. How are you, as a believer, able to recognize them? Jesus said:

Therefore by their fruits you [shall] know them.
Matthew 7:20

Yet, how many times have we heard some well-intended, misinformed saint of God begin to bind the spirit of witchcraft, or adultery, alcohol, tobacco, drugs, or some other spirit? There are no such spirits. If you read the text in Galatians 5:19-21, you will see that these are *"works of the flesh,"* or a manifestation of what the actual demon controlling the person is doing.

You cannot bind the flesh or the works of the flesh, because these actions are the results of the free will of a man. If you could bind them, God would have taken authority over what Adam and Eve were doing in the garden of Eden. He didn't. He would not over-ride the free will of the man to make his own choices.

The Holy Spirit warned Moses and the children of Israel in Deuteronomy 18:9:

When you come into the land which the LORD your God is giving you, you shall not learn to follow the abominations of those nations.

However, they forgot the warnings of God and DID learn to do all of the things that God forbade them to do. In today's society, we see all the more what (and why) God commanded the children of Israel (and the Church) not to learn or practice and not to live in these abominations.

Even in the Church today, we see these practices taking place without a thought. Why? Because the pastors have not been taught the Word of God. Instead, they have been taught the philosophy of the denomination they represent and its doctrines, and they ignore the Word. We are seeing witchcraft, magic, astrology, prognostication, whispering (ventriloquism in puppet shows), calling up the dead (a séance), reading the daily horoscopes, and many other forms of ungodliness all being accepted as good. God has no pleasure or part in these activities, and He does not accept them. He hates them.

Let's look at some of the manifestations in the flesh or, as I refer to them, "cohorts" that we can expect to see with this general of Satan:

Fortuneteller-Soothsayer: Someone who tries to tell the future by means of or use of familiar spirits (see Micah 5:12 and Isaiah 2:6)

WARLOCK, WITCH, WITCH DOCTOR, OR SORCERER: A male/female person involved in devil worship and casting spells (see Exodus 22:18, Leviticus 19:31, 20:6 and 1 Samuel 15:23)

HYPNOTIST-ENCHANTER: Mind Control (see Deuteronomy 18:11 and Isaiah 19:3)

REBELLION/WITCHCRAFT: A spirit of haughtiness (another of Satan's generals we will look at later), to resist authority, both God's and man's (see 1 Samuel 15:22-23)

STARGAZER-ZODIAC, HOROSCOPES: An attempt to predict the future by consulting the stars (see Isaiah 47:13, Leviticus 19:26 and Jeremiah 10:2)

WATER WITCHING: An attempt to find water with the aid of familiar spirits (another of Satan's generals), use of a dousing rod or forked willow branch (see Hosea 4:12)

MAGIC: An illusion or slight of hand trick used in order to deceive a person or audience (see Exodus 7:11, 8:7 and 9:11). Satan is a liar, a duplicator, and a deceiver.

DRUGS-HALLUCINOGENS: The use of an artificial stimulant, such as LSD, peyote, etc, to try to foretell the future (see Galatians 5:20, Revelation 9:21, 18:23, 21:8 and 22:15).[2]

Many of these manifestations of the spirit of divination are seen regularly in the churches of today, and no one seems to regard them as evil. They are accepted practices in the church. These are the very things God instructed Moses and the children of Israel NOT to learn or do. Yet, the church and individuals who call themselves Christians are practicing them, and they wonder why their prayers are not being answered.

The Word of God says in Isaiah 59:1-2:

> *Behold, the LORD's hand is not shortened*
> *That it cannot save;*
> *Nor His ear heavy,*
> *That it cannot hear.*
> *But your iniquities have separated you from*
> *your God;*
> *And your sins have hidden His face from you,*
> *So that He will not hear.*

This is one of the main reasons there is no power in

2. We see the definition for this word *drugs* in the Greek as *pharmacia*, where we get our word *pharmacy*, which also means "SORCERY." The judgment for it and its use are later found in the book of Revelation.

the church today. The younger members in particular are looking for something that will give them power and authority over their enemies. Little do they know that they are playing right into Satan's hands.

We have ministered to many who exhibit these signs and have had them say to us, "I'm okay. This is my gift and calling from God." Many are practicing witchcraft in the church and don't even realize it. How many times have you said or heard someone say they would "put a bug" in a particular person's [the pastor's or deacon's] ear? This is nothing short of mind control. When you become the instrument of influence in the life of another person, you have assumed the role of God the Holy Spirit. This is demonic.

Look at the results of Satan trying to assume the role of God. He was defeated, kicked out of Heaven, and lost all of his duties, authority, beauty, and eternal life with God, the Creator in Heaven. Is it that important for you to do the same thing and lose all of the same things, just as Satan did? DO NOT learn to do after the abominations of the inhabitants of the land.

Evil spirits have authority in rank with Satan. Just as in an army, there is rank, whether in the Kingdom of God, on earth, or in Satan's kingdom. Matthew 12:25-26 says:

But Jesus knew their thoughts, and said to them,

"Every kingdom divided against itself is brought to desolation, and every city or house divided against itself [shall] not stand. If Satan casts out Satan, he is divided against himself. How then will his kingdom stand?"

Jesus knew of the authority in rank. Why? Because this is how Heaven operates. There is the Father, the Son, and the Holy Ghost. This is how our chain of command in government and military also operates: The President, Vice-President, and Speaker of the House of Representatives. Under these offices are other offices, as well as the Secretary of Defense and various generals in command of the military.

In Satan's kingdom, there is also authority in rank, with Satan, the false prophet, and the anti-Christ, and various strongmen and lesser unclean spirits and imps as well. They all receive their orders in the same way, from the top down. It is the right and privilege of the true Church of Jesus to be able to "bind up" these servants of Satan and cancel their assignments, sending them back to the pit of Hell.

This is what was happening when Jesus was talking about binding the strongman (doorkeeper) in Matthew 12:28-29:

But if I cast out demons by the Spirit of God,

28

*surely the kingdom of God has come upon you.
Or how can one enter a strong man's house
and plunder his goods, unless he FIRST binds
the strong man? And then he will plunder his
house.* (Emphasis Mine)

Jesus has given us the authority to bind the strong-man and set his captives free or "plunder" his house and his goods. Jesus even went a step further in Mark 9:25. There He commanded the unclean spirit to never enter the man again.

Spiritual warfare is doing battle with the enemy and taking authority over his works and words. Let's look at some of the manifestations of demonic activity and presence from the Word.

In Matthew 17:18, we see no physical manifesta-tions. Jesus merely rebuked the demon, and it came out of the child. He was healed, or cured, from that very hour.

*And when he [the demon] saw Him [Jesus], the
spirit convulsed him [the child], and he fell to
the ground and wallowed, foaming at the mouth.*
Mark 9:20

With this young boy, we see the demonic activity

in the form of being thrown to the ground and foaming at the mouth (much like an attack of epilepsy).

Here's another case:

> *Now it happened on the next day, when they had come down from the mountain, that a great multitude met Him. Suddenly a man from the multitude cried out, saying, "Teacher, I implore you, look on my son, for he is my only child. And behold, a spirit seizes him, and he suddenly cries out; it convulses him so that he foams at the mouth; and it departs from him with great difficulty, bruising him. So I implored your disciples to cast it out, but they could not."*
>
> *Then Jesus answered and said, "O faithless and perverse generation, how long shall I be with you and bear with you? Bring your son here." As he was still coming, the demon threw him down and convulsed him. Then Jesus rebuked the unclean spirit, healed the child, and gave him back to his father.*   Luke 9:37-42

Again, we see the same scenario of the demon bruising the child, along with convulsions, foaming at the mouth, and the child being thrown to the ground. Here is another case:

> *Jesus asked him, saying, "What is your name?"*
> *And he said, "Legion," because many demons*
> *had entered him.*
> *And they begged Him that He would not com-*
> *mand them to go out into the abyss.*
>
> Luke 8:30-31

In this case, the demons talked back to Jesus when He asked their name.

Janice and I have been in the ministry of deliverance since December of 1979, and we have seen all of these and many more manifestations of demonic activity in persons we were ministering to. We have seen them slither on the floor like a snake with the tongue flickering in and out, others licking the dust from the floor, loud uncontrolled screams, vomiting, belching, passing gas, hiccups, trying to spit on us, throwing five-gallon cans of paint like thimbles, growling, and even trying to cut themselves and us with box cutters. These are all signs of demonic activity.

What do you do when ministering deliverance to a person who has exhibited the characteristics, or manifestations, of demonic activity?

FIRST: Cover yourself and others present with

the blood of Jesus for divine protection against this unclean spirit entering you and someone else present. Ask this person if they are a Christian. If not, lead them in the sinner's prayer, asking God to forgive them of their sins and asking Jesus into their lives, to be their Lord and Savior.

SECOND: Bind the unclean spirits from the "tearing" of the individual being ministered to. You are taking authority over the spirits present and subjugating them to the name, blood, and power of Jesus.

> *But made Himself of no reputation, taking the form of a bondservant, and coming in the likeness of men. And being found in appearance as a man, He humbled Himself and became obedient to the point of death, even the death of the cross. Therefore God also has highly exalted Him and given Him the name which is above every name, that at the name of Jesus every knee should bow, of those in heaven, and of those on earth, and of those under the earth, and that every tongue should confess that Jesus Christ is Lord, to the glory of God the Father.* Philippians 2:7-11

This is your right and privilege as a child of

God. Jesus has given us the right to use His name in casting out demons (see Mark 16:17-18). Use your right as a citizen of Heaven and do combat against the devil and his forces.

What happens to these unclean spirits when they leave? The spirit leaves the person and goes to a dry place for a season, as seen in Matthew 12:43-45 and also in Luke:

> *When an unclean spirit goes out of a man, he goes through dry places, seeking rest; and finding none, he says, "I will return to my house from which I came." And when he comes, he finds it swept and put in order [garnished, KJV]. Then he goes and takes with him seven other spirits more wicked than himself, and they enter and dwell there; and the last state of that man is worse than the first.* Luke 11:24-26

This is why Jesus spoke to the unclean spirits and told them not enter back into the young man after he was delivered. This is so very important when ministering to others. You DO NOT want that spirit (or those spirits) to return. Why? Because the latter condition of that person will be seven times worse than in the beginning. This is also why it is so important to have them filled with the Holy Ghost, to prevent the spirit (or spirits) from returning.

If you look at verse 25, it says *"when he [the evil spirit] comes, he finds it swept and [garnished]."* *"Swept and garnished"* here literally means "religiously decorated." This house looks pretty and clean inside, but nothing has been added to fill the void left by the exit of the demonic spirit. This vacancy MUST be filled with the Spirit of God. If not, the same old resident will come back and take up residency again, this time with seven of his buddies, and the end result will be devastation and death (both in the natural and in the spiritual).

So now that we have identified the unclean spirit by his works and manifestation in the flesh (see Matthew 7:20), what do we do next? Bind up the spirit of divination, not the works of the flesh. Remember: in the beginning of the chapter I said that the works of the flesh cannot be bound. They are free-will acts of the person, but they are controlled by demonic spirits that can and must be bound in order to set the person free. Also remember what Jesus said in Mark 16:17:

And these signs shall follow them that believe: In my name shall they cast out devils; they shall speak with new tongues. (KJV)

What does the word *shall* mean? In my book, *The Authority of the Believer*, we found that this word is a legal term meaning "mandatory obligation to be carried out and fulfilled." Jesus, speaking in this verse, has placed Heaven under mandatory obligation to carry out (or fulfill) this request from His children. Jesus also gave us a promise in Matthew 16:19 and 18:18:

Whatever you bind on earth will be bound in heaven, and whatever you loose on earth will be loosed in heaven.

Believe it and act on it!

THIRD: Now that the spirit of divination has been bound with the authority of the Word of God and the blood of Jesus, what's next? According to Matthew 18:18, you must loose the Holy Spirit and the gifts of the Spirit to the person you are ministering to. These gifts can be found in 1 Corinthians 12:8-11.

— FOR YOUR NOTES—

_____

_____

_____

_____

_____

_____

_____

_____

_____

_____

_____

_____

_____

_____

CHAPTER 2

FAMILIAR SPIRIT

DEFINITION: *"To make known, to know, to ascertain by seeing, to observe through acquaintance of an unclean spirit."*

NOTE: The works of the flesh cannot be bound. They are free-will acts of the person, but they are controlled by demonic spirits that can and must be bound in order to set the person free. Galatians 5:19-21 gives a glimpse of the works of the flesh, which are manifested and that we see in operation in the spiritually possessed or oppressed.

This is another of Satan's generals or "strongmen" used against the Body of Christ to destroy us or make us ineffective. I call this general "The Family Liar." Satan has assigned one of these spirits to each of us in order to track our every move and to get "familiar" with us. The goal is to use the knowledge gained about us against us.

Do you ever wonder why so many people continue to call the local psychic or medium for advice and get some form of prediction? How do such people know anything about us, having never met us? It is with the aid of this demon spirit from Hell. Satan has used the information he gleaned about you to deceive you. With that deception, he hopes that you will make a very grave mistake so that he can kill you (both spiritually and physically).

Let's look at some of the manifestations, or works, of the flesh associated with this general and how to recognize him.

> *By their fruits ye shall know them.*
> Matthew 7:20, KJV

NECROMANCER: A person who claims to tell the future by allegedly communicating with the dead (see Deuteronomy 18:11)

MEDIUM: A person through whom communication comes from the dead (1 Samuel 28:8-19 gives an example of this in the story of Saul and his contact with the witch of Endor).

SPIRITIST: A person who communicates with the dead (see 1 Samuel 28: 8-19, concerning Samuel and the witch of Endor)

YOGA: A practice involving intense and complete concentration upon something, especially an unclean deity, in order to establish an identity of consciousness with the object of concentration (see Jeremiah 29:8)

PASSIVE MIND DREAMERS: A person who offers no opposition or restraint, an impractical person, a visionary of the wrong sort (see Jeremiah 23:16, 25, 32 and 27:9-10)

FALSE PROPHECY: Not accurate or true, not from God (see Isaiah 8:19, 29:4 and Ezekiel 13:17-23)

PEEPING AND MUTTERING [VENTRILOQUISM]: To speak in low indistinct tones without lip movement, to complain, grumble; Latin meaning "belly talk" (see Isaiah 8:19, 29:4 and 59:3)

DRUGS-HALLUCINOGENS: A narcotic, habit-forming drug used as an aid to perceive sight, sounds, etc., not present, aided by drugs, Greek *pharmacia*, meaning "sorcery" (see Revelation 9:21, 18:23, 21:8, 22:15 and Galatians 5:20)

CLAIRVOYANT: The ability to perceive things that are not in sight, or which cannot be seen (see 1 Samuel 28:7-8)

These are some of the manifestations of this general of Satan, and it was for this very reason that God instructed Moses and the children of Israel as He did in Deuteronomy 18:9-14:

When you come into the land which the LORD your God is giving you, you shall not learn to follow the abominations of those nations.
Verse 9

God saw these nations who inhabited the Promised Land as ungodly, heathen people who were serving false gods, not Him. In a word study, these inhabitants are also referred to as "a troop of heathens or pack of wild animals." This is why God instructed the children of Israel NOT to learn their practices. He is also instructing us, as the Church of today, NOT to learn the practices of the modern world. These practices are against what God has required of us in 1 Peter 2:9:

But you are a chosen generation, a royal priest-hood, a holy nation, His own special people, that you may proclaim the praises of Him who called you out of darkness into His marvelous light.

We are a chosen people, just as the children of Israel were, chosen to serve the living God and NOT His creation or creatures. God has called us to a very special mission on this earth, to point the lost of this world to Him and show the glory of God in our lives before them. We are the children of the King and must walk like the royal children we are.

As Janice noted in her foreword, in 2007, she and I were privileged to sit and allow King Shirinda of Limpopo Province, South Africa, to teach us what it means to be the child of a king. This man is the son of a king, and is now a king in his own right. He is also an attorney and a judge. Most important of all, he is a child of the King of Kings and a man filled with the Holy Spirit. He knows who and what he is and walks in all of these offices with the utmost of confidence.

Everything King Shirinda is in the natural, he also is in the Spirit. When he speaks, his subjects listen to and obey him. Why? Because he has authority in his kingdom. He also speaks into the Spirit realm and has unclean spirits obey him. Why? Because he knows his authority, he walks where God has placed him in this earth, and he is fulfilling the roll of chosen generation, royal priesthood, and holy nation. Sadly, too many of us of the modern church have no idea who (or what) we are in Jesus or His Kingdom. We have learned the practices of the heathen of this land and allowed them into the church, even implementing some of their practices ourselves.

"What practices," you might ask, "have we allowed into the church and called it good or okay and used it to reach the children?" In Chapter 1, we looked at the spirit of divination. Part of that was dealing with the practices in Deuteronomy 18:9-14, and, in particular, ventriloquism or "throwing your voice," or its translation from Latin, "belly talk." We are allowing this practice, with puppet shows, magicians, and magic shows, into the church to "entertain" our children.

This is the same conduct as the worshippers of Baal, offering up their children to this demonic god. In this way, we are training our children to see no problem with divination or any of the works of the flesh that are associated with it, such as rebellion, witchcraft, and any of the others found in Galatians 5:19-21. All of these are an abomination to God, as He stated in Deuteronomy 18:12:

For all who do these things are an abomination to the LORD, and because of these abominations the LORD your God drives them out from before you.

What does the word *abomination* mean? According to the *American Heritage Dictionary of the English Language*, abomination is defined as "abhorrence for someone or something; loathing; something that elicits great dislike or abhorrence." In other words, God has a great dislike for these practices. He is a jealous God and does not allow our praise and worship to be given to another god of lower rank than Himself. This is what happens when we practice the rituals of the heathen.

When God says, "Don't do it," He means just that. Look at Saul in 1 Samuel 28:8-19. He went to the witch of Endor and asked her to perform a séance and call up the spirit of Samuel. Why? Because he needed instruction about the battle he was in. The witch did what he asked and then realized who he was and what he had done to her. It was a Jewish, God-authored law that a witch was to be stoned to death. They were not allowed to live, and Saul was making a deal with a witch that he would not carry out the prescribed punishment handed down by

God's Law. He was compromising the statutes of the Lord and also of his office as king. And because he had compromised, God was very angry with him.

But how many pastors in the modern church have compromised their offices, just as Saul did? They have allowed the same forms of witchcraft and other ungodly, forbidden practices into the church and embraced them as good.

What was the punishment for Saul asking this woman to call on a familiar spirit? In 1 Chronicles 10:13-14, we see that the proscribed punishment was actually death, and Saul died prematurely because of it:

> *So Saul died for his unfaithfulness which he had committed against the LORD, because he did not keep the Word of the LORD, and also because he consulted a medium for guidance.* Verse 13

> *Therefore say to the house of Israel, "This is what the Sovereign LORD says: Repent! Turn from your idols and renounce all your detestable practices!*
> *"When any of the Israelites or any foreigner residing in Israel separate themselves from me and set up idols in their hearts and put a wicked stumbling block before their faces and then go*

to a prophet to inquire of me, I the LORD will answer them myself. I will set my face against them and make them an example and a byword. I will remove them from my people. Then you will know that I am the LORD.

"And if the prophet is enticed to utter a prophecy, I the LORD have enticed that prophet, and I will stretch out my hand against him and destroy him from among my people Israel. They will bear their guilt—the prophet will be as guilty as the one who consults him. Then the people of Israel will no longer stray from me, nor will they defile themselves anymore with all their sins. They will be my people, and I will be their God, declares the Sovereign LORD."

Ezekiel 14:6-11, NIV

As noted previously, the works of the flesh are spelled out in Galatians 5:

Now the works of the flesh are evident, which are: adultery, fornication, uncleanness, lewdness, idolatry, sorcery, hatred, contentions, jealousies, outbursts of wrath, selfish ambitions, dissensions, heresies, envy, murders, drunkenness, revelries, and the like; of which I tell you beforehand, just as I also told you in time past, that those who practice such things [shall] not inherit the kingdom of God. Galatians 5:19-21

God also said in Deuteronomy 30:9:

I call heaven and earth as witnesses today against you, that I have set before you life and death, blessing and cursing; therefore choose life, that both you and your descendants may live.

Also see Exodus 22:18 and Leviticus 19:31 and 20:6.

What can be done if we have been associated with, or practiced some of these activities? For every man and woman, boy and girl, there is forgiveness in the name of Jesus and His blood. All we are required to do is ask for it. Romans 3:23 says:

For ALL have sinned and fall short of the glory of God. (Emphasis Mine)

Romans 6:23 says:

For the wages of sin is death, but the gift of God is eternal life in Christ Jesus our Lord.

John 3:16 says:

46

For God so loved the world that He gave His only begotten Son, that whoever believes in Him should not perish but have everlasting life.

According to the Word of God, all of us have sinned or missed the mark of God's high calling for our lives. But He has made a way for us to be redeemed back to Him. This applies even to the person or persons involved in the many occultic practices of Satan.

Now that we have learned that allowing this general of Satan to operate in our lives or the lives of someone we are ministering to brings death, what must we do?

FIRST: Cover yourself and anyone else present with the blood of Jesus for divine protection. Ask if the person is a Christian. If not, lead them in the sinner's prayer, asking God for forgiveness of their sins and asking Jesus into their lives as their Lord and Savior.

SECOND: Bind the familiar spirit (not the works of the flesh) and cast him out of the person. Why do we not bind the works of the flesh? Because they are the free-will acts of a free-willed person and cannot be bound. However, as you bind the "general or

47

strongman," you may also bind his cohorts that are with him.

What is a *cohort?* According to the *American Heritage Dictionary of the English Language*, a cohort is "a companion or associate." I have dealt with demons many times and have seen all of the works of the flesh disappear when the "strongman" has left. He takes with him the desires to continue doing those works of the flesh. This is what Jesus was saying when He said we are to *"plunder [take the goods from]"* the strongman's house (Matthew 12:29).

Mark 16:17-18 declares:

> *These signs will accompany those who have believed: in My name they will cast out demons, they will speak in new tongues; they will pick up serpents, and if they drink any deadly poison, it will not harm them; they will lay hands on the sick, and they will recover.* (NASB)

In the Old English of the King James Version, the word *shall* is used instead of *will. Shall,* again, means, "a mandatory obligation to be carried out or fulfilled." This word has more authority or power a simple *will.*

Jesus said:

Behold, I give you the authority to trample on serpents and scorpions, and over all the power of the enemy, and nothing shall by any means hurt you. Luke 10:19

Now that the familiar spirit and his cohorts have been bound in the life of the person being ministered to, what's next?

THIRD: Now loose The Holy Spirit and the gifts of the Spirit according to 1 Corinthians 12:9-12, allowing Him to bring the healing and deliverance to the person. Why do I say "healing?" Because this person has had a traumatic sickness in their life and body and now needs physical healing as well. By releasing the Holy Spirit with the gifts of the Spirit, you are asking Him to bring the covenant Jesus bought and paid for with the stripes on His back to this person for healing of spirit, soul (mind, will, and emotions), and body.

As I mentioned, lead them in the prayer of salvation, but then ask God to fill them with His Holy Spirit so that the house of the former resident is now occupied by the Spirit of God. This also gives the person power to live a victorious life and to discern unclean spirits that will try to control them in the future.

AUTHORITY: *"Delegated power, right to command, to enforce obedience, to make final decisions OVER THE ENEMY."*

— FOR YOUR NOTES —

— FOR YOUR NOTES—

CHAPTER 3

SPIRIT OF JEALOUSY

DEFINITION: *"Resentfully suspicious of a rival or rivals influence; demanding excessive loyalty, resentfully envious; to have hatred or ill will because of another's advantages, possessions, religion, or race."*

NOTE: Again I want to remind you that the works of the flesh cannot be bound. They are free-will acts of the person, but they are controlled by demonic spirits that can and must be bound in order to set the person free. Once more, Galatians 5:19-21 gives us a glimpse of these works of the flesh that we can identify in the life of persons being oppressed or possessed by the devil.

NOTE: As we deal with these strongmen or generals of Satan, you will see that there is no "Spirit of Jezebel." There is, however, the spirit that she operated under—jealousy,

which can control either male or female. It controlled both Jezebel and her husband, Ahab (see 1 Kings 21: 2-16).

Once more, recall God's instruction to Moses and the children of Israel in Deuteronomy 18:9:

> *When you come into the land which the LORD your God is giving you, you SHALL NOT learn to follow the abominations of those nations.* (My Emphasis)

Look at the definition of the word *heathen*: "A foreign nation or a troop of animals" (see Ephesians 5:3-11, Deuteronomy 12:29-30 and Galatians 5:19-21).

Let's look at some of the works of the flesh under this general or strongman. Again, how do you recognize him? Matthew 7:20 states, *"By their fruits you [shall] know them."* Jesus is saying that we will recognize the spirit by what it is producing on the outside of the person, by what that person is doing or how they are acting in the natural. Here are some things to look for:

MURDER: The unlawful and malicious or premeditated killing of another human being (see Genesis 4:8, Exodus 20:13 and Matthew 5:21-22)

REVENGE-SPITE: To inflict damage, injury, or punishment for the same as that which was done to you, to get even (see Proverbs 6:34 and 14:16-17)

CRUELTY: Someone who is inclined to inflict pain or suffering; delighting in another's pain (see Song of Solomon 8:6 and Proverbs 27:4)

CAUSING DIVISIONS: To cause a dividing or separation, to cause disagreement or strife between individuals; i.e. members of a family, church, business, etc. (see Galatians 5:20)

JEALOUSY: A feeling that may result in harm or injury to another (see Song of Solomon 8:6)

ENVY: Hatred or ill will for another person or persons (see Proverbs 14:30 and Galatians 5:21)

STRIFE: The act of striving or competing excessively with another, contentious, extreme competition, to be quarrelsome, conflict (see Proverbs 10:12 and Galatians 5:20)

CONTENTION: Verbal strife, arguing, quarreling, controversy (see Proverbs 13:10)

EXTREME COMPETITION: Extreme opposition toward another person, extreme rivalry (see Genesis 4:4-5)

HATE/PREJUDICE: Bad tempered, to have a strong dislike or ill will for another; to dislike or despise (see Genesis 37:3-4 and 8 and 1 Thessalonians 4:8)

ANGER/RAGE: Uncontrolled anger causing harm or injury (see Genesis 4:5-6, Proverbs 6:34, 14:29, 22:24-25 and 29:22-23)

As you look at the works of the flesh here, you can see why I said that there is no spirit of Jezebel, but only the strongman or general that controlled her and Ahab. You can see all of the manifestations of this general in her. She was envious, angry, jealous of other's property and possessions, and she caused divisions between Ahab and the subjects of his kingdom, all which ultimately lead to murder.

We see this spirit in the lives of many people in the world today, including our own elected officials. It always leads to the same ultimate end — death, the death of someone, of a culture, a system, and possibly of the person or persons being controlled by this strongman. This spirit has no gender requirements, as long as he can control and manipulate the person and ultimately destroy the gift God has placed in them for His glory.

This spirit is seen in the statement "the American Dream." What is behind this statement? All too often, it is greed. "I want to heap to myself all the material possession I can." Many will lie, cheat, steal, and make a deal with the devil to make this come true in their lives.

Don't get me wrong: I don't have a problem with having material possessions. What I have a problem with is the fact that the possessions too often control and own you rather than you controlling or owning them. You have no freedom to do with them or use them as you should.

Many years ago, I had a problem with owning guns. I would buy a new one every year right before hunting season would open here in Louisiana. I was addicted to owning more guns. One year, I traded an old P08, World War II 9 MM German Luger for a new shotgun to replace one that had been stolen from me a few years earlier. I had been hunting with a double-barreled, black-powder shotgun until that time. But then I took a member of my church hunting one Saturday morning, and the Holy Spirit instructed me to take the black-powder shotgun and give the semi-automatic to my church member.

I felt like Abraham offering up Isaac on the altar. This semi-automatic shotgun was the best shotgun I had ever owned.

That morning, when we arrived at the hunting spot, my church member pulled out an old bolt-action 20-gauge shotgun to hunt with. I handed him my semi-auto and told him to hunt with it that morning. He argued with me, but I insisted that he hunt with it. I hunted with the black-powder shotgun instead.

I had a blast hunting squirrels that morning. I actually took my limit, and he only saw and took a few. When he handed the gun back to me, I said, "No, this is yours now. The Holy Spirit has instructed me to give it to you." Since that day, I own the guns; they don't own me. God broke that spirit of jealousy and his works in my life simply by me being obedient to the Father.

I have seen this spirit in the lives of many people we minister to in the church. They want to live the "dream," but they get caught up in the lifestyle of "possessing things." Often, their things possess them. The Word of God does not say that money is the root of all evil. It is the love of or lusting after money that is the root of all evil.

For the love of money is a root of all kinds of evil, for which some have strayed from the faith in their greediness, and pierced themselves through with many sorrows. 1 Timothy 6:10

God is saying that uncontrolled greed for money (or anything else) is the root of all types of evil. Look at Jezebel and her lust and greed for other men's possessions. What was her final outcome? She was thrown from the second-story window of the palace, and the dogs ate her body, with the exception of her hands, feet, and head.

What does that say to us about those dogs? They didn't want to touch the blood of those defiled hands, those feet that had carried Jezebel into places of ungodliness, or the head (the soul) that had been controlled by this demon spirit from Hell.

What does it benefit or profit a man if he gains all the money in the world through the works, or control, of this demon and then loses his own soul in the bargain? The ultimate goal of Jezebel and her husband was to become "filthy rich," no matter what the cost or who they hurt in the process.

Jealousy is running rampant in the modern church. Many pastors are just trying to outdo the church down the block or across town. In the process, they are building their own monuments, or legacies, of success, instead of building the Kingdom of God.

Deacons are trying to control the pastor and everything that is done in the church, while overlooking the call and responsibilities God has placed on them. Members, who have been in the congregation for decades or who built the church building, think they have "the right" to tell the pastor or elder off, as is found in 1 Timothy 5:1-2. They feel justified in telling him what to do whenever they like. This is touching God's anointed man or woman, whom He has ordained as shepherd or elder in that church.

I have seen this first-hand. It happened to me, and it was done by someone the Holy Spirit classified as a "pipsqueak Jezebel." Greed, strife, jealousy, contention, envy, anger and divisions ... these are the fruits of this evil spirit.

This is the very reason there are churches on every street corner in every nation of the world that are only half full and not meeting the needs of their congregations. The members come in sick, hurting, rejected, financially broke, and dying from diseases, and they leave the same way they came in. When they go to the church for help, they're told, "We don't pray for the sick anymore; that passed away with the original disciples." Well, praise God, it has not passed away: I am a disciple of Jesus. How about you?

When pastors are asked for financial help, they respond, "We're not a lending institution." Yet they turn around and build a multi-million dollar building with some lame excuse. And for what? It serves their own self-esteem and pride. When pastors are asked for deliverance by a member, they say, "I don't know how to do that," or "We don't believe in that." When those pastors are asked by members of the church to allow Janice and myself to come and teach the congregation or just certain members about deliverance and spiritual warfare, they are either put off or given an outright "NO." This is nothing but jealousy.

I have been in the ministry since 1959, licensed in the Baptist Church and ordained into the Full Gospel. I have pastored my own church, ministered in and with the Assemblies of God and others, ministered with many nationally-known ministers and music artists, and ministered in many states and in foreign countries. I started many churches, ordained many ministers and others into the ministry of helps.

I was saved at the age of six, on February 18, 1951, and filled with the Holy Ghost with the evidence of speaking in other tongues. God has also used me in the office of a prophet.

I earned my Ph.D. in Biblical Studies, and yet I was told by a young pastor that I could not minister in his church because I had not "paid my dues" to be allowed to do so. Oddly, I was his father's associate pastor for years. Again, this is nothing but jealousy and control.

God said through Hosea the prophet:

> *My people are destroyed for lack of knowledge.*
> *Because you have rejected knowledge,*
> *I also will reject you from being priest for Me;*
> *Because you have forgotten the law of your God,*
> *I also will forget your children.*   Hosea 4:6

God's people are being destroyed for their lack of knowledge, and it is the ministers (pastors) who are standing in the way of the knowledge of God being brought into the churches. This does not make sense to me in any way. I thought we were all working for the same thing, depopulating Hell and populating Heaven, bring lost people to the saving knowledge and understanding of Jesus. Whether we are Baptists, Methodists, Assemblies of God, Pentecostals, Catholics, Presbyterians, or whatever the name over the door is, it's all to be done in the name of Jesus and for Jesus Christ and His Kingdom. If He's not in it, then we're wasting our time.

In 1 Corinthians 1:10-17, Paul was talking to the church about sectarianism and showed that it is a sin:

Now I plead with you, brethren, by the name of our Lord Jesus Christ, that you all speak the same thing and that there be no divisions among you, but that you be perfectly joined together in the same mind and in the same judgment. For it has been declared to me concerning you, my brethren, by those of Chloe's household, that there are contentions among you. Now I say this, that each of you says, "I am of Paul," or "I am of Apollos," or "I am of Cephas," or "I am of Christ." Is Christ divided? Was Paul crucified for you? Or were you baptized in the name of Paul?

I thank God that I baptized none of you except Crispus and Gaius, lest anyone should say that I had baptized in my own name. Yes, I also baptized the household of Stephanas. Besides, I do not know whether I baptized any other. For Christ did not send me to baptize, but to preach the gospel, not with wisdom of words, lest the cross of Christ should be made of no effect.

What is the definition of this word *sectarianism*? The *American Heritage Dictionary of the English Language* defines it in this way: "pertaining to or characteristic of a sect or sects. Adhering to or confined to the dogmatic limits of the sect. Narrow minded; parochial. A member of a sect. One characterized by bigoted adherence to a factional viewpoint."

Denominations were not and are not an idea put forth by Jesus. He wanted all of us to dwell in peace and harmony with each other and have all things in common, even in our understanding of the Word and our commitment to Him as our Lord and Savior. Here is where the devil entered the religious realm and began to divide and conquer the Church of Jesus Christ, and he did it with divisions, jealousies, and contentions.

We taught Spiritual Warfare and the Believer at Zion Hill Family Church in Pineville, Louisiana, where Dr. Joshua Joy Dara is the Senior Pastor. At the end of the sixteen weeks of class, his response to it all was this: "It is desperately needed by the Body of Christ to educate and inform us." We saw many lives changed through the teaching there. Many people were healed and delivered from demonic oppression. Why is this not being taught elsewhere? It's because of jealousy, plain and simple.

Janice and I have a very unique calling on our lives, and unfortunately, many people, including pastors, don't understand that call or us, and therefore, we have been shunned. We have seen the "heathen or troop of animals" in the church and, for the most part, they control it.

Jesus classified jealousy, or equated it, with murder. Matthew 5:21-22 and Ephesians 4:25-32 both say basically the same thing regarding jealousy, anger, bitterness, wrath, clamor, and evil speaking. He said to put aside all of this in verse 31, then concludes:

> *And be kind to one another, tenderhearted, forgiving one another, even as God in Christ forgave you.* Ephesians 4:32

Jesus said in Matthew 5:21-22:

> *You have heard that it was said to those of old, "You shall not murder, and whoever murders will be in danger of the judgment." But I say to you that whoever is angry with his brother without a cause shall be in danger of the judgment. And whoever says to his brother, "Raca!" shall be in danger of the council. But whoever says, "You fool!" shall be in danger of hell fire.*

Murder is one of the manifestations, or "cohorts," of the flesh signifying the presence of this general or strongman of Satan. This is where it starts, in the heart of the man brought on by jealousy, envy, and strife.

What is the punishment for operating in or under the influence of this demon, or any demon, for that matter? Galatians 5:21 states:

> *I tell you beforehand, just as I also told you in time past, that those who practice such things shall not inherit the kingdom of God.*

The Holy Spirit is telling us here that if we continue to allow this demonic general to control our lives and we live in these manifestations, we SHALL NOT inherit (come into possession of) the Kingdom of God. That is very cut and dried.

> *For the wages of sin is death, but the gift of God is eternal life in Christ Jesus our Lord.*
> Romans 6:23

Payment for sin is death ... but God! God has made a way for us through the blood of Jesus. When we come to Jesus and admit our sins and ask Him for forgiveness for what we have done and ask Him to wash us clean in His blood, He does just that. He washes away our sins and makes us clean and white.

Even more wonderful, He never again remembers those sins against us.

When we encounter people under the influence of the spirit of jealousy who want to be free, what should we do?

FIRST: Cover yourself and any other person or persons present with the blood of Jesus for divine protection. Ask the person needing prayer if they are a Christian. If not, lead them in the sinner's prayer, asking God for forgiveness of their sins and asking Jesus into their lives to be their Lord and Savior

SECOND: Now, bind the spirit of jealousy and his cohorts (not the works of the flesh) and command it to come out of the person. Jesus said:

> *And I will give you the keys of the kingdom of heaven, and whatever you bind on earth will be bound in heaven, and whatever you loose on earth will be loosed in heaven.* Matthew 16:19
> (See also see Matthew 18:18, Mark 16:17 and Luke 10:19.)

Bind this strongman, or general, and command it in the name of Jesus to loose and leave this person in the name of Jesus. Remember, every name that is named in Heaven, earth, or under the earth is subject to the name of Jesus, and therefore they must obey.

THIRD: Now guide this individual in prayer, asking for the infilling of the Holy Spirit to enable them to live an overcoming life. Remember, the old tenant is now gone and a new tenant, the Holy Spirit, must occupy this house in order for it to remain free of the old tenant. Loose the Spirit of the love of God (the Holy Spirit).

1 Corinthians 13 and Ephesians 5:2 both refer to the love of Christ. As we loose the love of God (His Holy Spirit) into the lives of the individual, this helps them begin to love others where they once were controlled by Satan's general.

Do all of this through the authority Jesus has given you.

AUTHORITY: "Delegated power, right to command, to enforce obedience, to make final decisions over the enemy."

— For Your Notes —

— For Your Notes—

CHAPTER 4

LYING SPIRIT

DEFINITION: *"To tell lies, falsehoods, or untruths about another."*

NOTE: The works of the flesh cannot be bound. They are free-will acts of the person, but they are controlled by demonic spirits that can and must be bound in order to set the person free. Again, Galatians 5:19-21 gives us a glimpse of these works of the flesh that we can identify in the life of people being oppressed or possessed by the devil.

As we look at this general, or strongman, of Satan, we will see many characteristics or manifestations of it in everyday life, family life, business life, and, yes, even in church life. You might ask, "But how can this strongman be in the church?" Let's take a look at his works, or manifestations, and see if you can recognize him.

STRONG DECEPTIONS: The act or practice of deceiving, an illusion, not real (see 2 Thessalonians 2:9-12)

FLATTERY: Excessive untruth, insincere praise (Jezebel in 2 Kings 9:30-37) (see also Psalm 78:36, Proverbs 20:19, 26:28 and 29:59)

FALSE PROPHECY: To declare or predict something that is not true as by divine influence or guidance (see Matthew 7:15-20, especially verse 15, Jeremiah 23:16-17, 27:9-10 and Ezekiel 13:17-18)

GOSSIP: A person who chatters or repeats idle talk or rumors about others (see 2 Timothy 2:16 and 1 Timothy 6:20)

LIES: Falsehoods, untruths (see Proverbs 6:16-19 and 2 Chronicles 18:22)

SLANDER: The spreading of false statements harmful to another's character or reputation (see Proverbs 10:16-18)

ACCUSATIONS: A criminal complaint, to charge with crime whether true or not (see Revelation 12:10 and Psalm 31:18)

FALSE TEACHERS: One who wrongfully instructs or teaches others and does it willingly (see 1 Timothy 4:1-3, 2 Timothy 4:3, 2 Peter 2:1 and Titus 1:11)

RELIGIOUS BONDAGE: To be enslaved, to be in subjection to some force by compulsion or strong influence (see Galatians 5:1-4 and 1 Corinthians 1:10-13)

SUPERSTITIONS: Any belief that is inconsistent with the known laws of science or what is generally known to be true (see 1 Timothy 4:7)

Now, do you see any of these manifestations operating in the local or national churches or church governing bodies? Yes, these are very prevalent in the church from the local level right up to the national and international levels. We can see all of these in operation on a daily basis. Some prominent lies that are circulating in the church are:

- "Healing passed away with the early disciples."
- "Speaking in tongues is of the devil."
- "You must, at all times, submit to your pastor, no matter what."
- "Prophecy is of the devil."

These and many more of this general's manifestations are evident today. I see churches in our own cities here in Central Louisiana that are filing lawsuits against their members and against the pastors because of the lies, strong deceptions, and gossip. Friends, this ought not to be.

Many of the practices of the heathen are being accepted and embraced by the church. Look at a major one that almost everyone celebrates every year: Mardi Gras and Fat Tuesday (the last day before Lent.) These are the last times to be able to sin before Lent. And what are the practices at Mardi Gras? Drinking, reveling, and all sorts of perversions. These were named specifically by Paul in Galatians 5:21:

> *... envy, murders, drunkenness, revelries, and the like; of which I tell you beforehand, just as I also told you in time past, that those who practice such things shall not inherit the kingdom of God.*

What was he talking about? Excessive drunkenness, boisterous or out-of-control partying, along with every sort of sexual perversion associated with them.

Many years ago, I witnessed a sad thing in a church in South Louisiana. The church was in the middle of a "revival," and the father of one of the member's died in another city. Because they were in revival, the pastor of the church refused to allow that member to go and bury her father. This is demonic control, religious bondage to the rules of an ungodly man.

Why do I say this man was ungodly? Because he was not operating in the love of Jesus and had no compassion for his member. What would Jesus have done? He would have gone with the member and raised the father from the dead, but this was beyond the scope of this pastor's thinking or ability. He was so self-centered he could not see the brokenness of the woman, nor did he know how to minister to her. At the same time, we were pastoring a church in which we saw the dead raised, blind eyes opened, cancers and tumors being healed, and many other such miracles from God.

Why were we seeing all of this happen? Because we were moving in God's love and compassion for His people, and we were seeing them with the same eyes as the Father, eyes of compassion, eyes of love, and eyes of mercy.

We have known of pastors who were at one time mighty men of God, but somewhere down the line they were seduced and drawn away from the truth of God's Word by believing the lies of the devil. Then, sadly, they began to teach false doctrine to their members. Some of these men and women are teaching that once you are saved you can do anything you desire to do. You are saved and nothing can change that. This is a lie from Satan called by some "ultimate reconciliation." Jesus said in Matthew 10:22:

> *He who endures to the end shall be saved.*
> (See also Matthew 24:13.)

There is a law of "much mention." When we see in the Word a statement or series of statements that are repeated more than once, the Holy Spirit is trying to teach us something. We must stop, look, and listen to what He is teaching us. Jesus said in Luke 9:

> *But Jesus said to him, "No one, having put his hand to the plow, and looking back, is fit for the kingdom of God."*   Luke 9:62

That's clear enough, but part of this general's assignment is to use his abilities to deceive the weaker

Christians into believing his lies—false teachings, false prophecies, strong deceptions.

I often put the word *pastors* in quotation marks. Why? Because there are many who are not called by the Holy Spirit who are using this venue as a money-making job for their own financial gains. Read Ezekiel 34 and see for yourselves what I'm referring to.

There are so many manifestations of this general, or strongman, which are too numerous to mention. All one needs to do is watch the lives of people, and you will see them. How do we recognize them? Jesus said:

> *Beware of false prophets, who come to you in sheep's clothing, but inwardly they are ravenous wolves. You will know them by their fruits. Do men gather grapes from thorn bushes or figs from thistles? Even so, every good tree bears good fruit, but a bad tree bears bad fruit. A good tree cannot bear bad fruit, nor can a bad tree bear good fruit. Every tree that does not bear good fruit is cut down and thrown into the fire. Therefore by their fruits you shall know them.*
> Matthew 7:15-20

By the fruit they produce you will recognize them. It takes much prayer in the Holy Ghost and submission to Him to be consistent in discerning this and other demonic spirits from Satan. Many say, "That is not my calling or ministry." It is every Christian's ministry to effectively and totally minister to the whole man—spirit, soul, and body. This is why we are here on this earth.

Jesus told us in Matthew 28:19-20:

> *GO THEREFORE [YOU GO and be My disciples], and make disciples of all nations, baptizing them in the name of the Father and of the Son and of the Holy Spirit, teaching them to observe all things that I have commanded you; and lo, I am with you always, even to the end of the age. Amen.* (Emphasis Mine)

This is what Jesus would do if He were here. Now He will do it through us because He is here in us.

I want to continue to remind you of the command God gave to Moses and the children of Israel in Deuteronomy 18:9:

> *When you come into the land which the LORD your God is giving you, you shall not learn to follow the abominations of those nations.*

You might be saying, "That's Old Testament and doesn't apply to us today." Okay, then let's look at Ephesians 5:11:

And have no fellowship with the unfruitful works of darkness, but rather expose them.

What parts of God's Word do you want to throw out and what parts do you want to believe? This is what the cults do. Either you believe that the entire Word of God, from Genesis 1:1 to Revelations 22:20, is completely infallible, without mistake, and is inspired by the Holy Spirit, or you believe none of it is, which makes you no better than the cultic heathen.

The Father takes a very dim view of liars. He compares liars with murderers, idolaters, whoremongers, and many other evil persons. Look how He compares them in Revelation 21:8:

But the cowardly, unbelieving, abominable, murderers, sexually immoral, sorcerers, idolaters, and all liars shall have their part in the lake which burns with fire and brimstone, which is the second death.

Revelation 22:15 says:

> *But outside are dogs and sorcerers and sexu-*
> *ally immoral and murderers and idolaters, and*
> *whoever loves and practices a lie.*

Proverbs 12:22 declares:

> *Lying lips are an abomination to the LORD,*
> *But those who deal truthfully are His delight.*

God has made His will known to us through His Word, and His Word does not change. He hates lying in any form. Still, we see it in the church today in the form of gossip, slander, false prophecy, false teachings, and many other forms.

Remember that lying is also another of Satan's generals (strongmen) that we have already exposed. Also, remember many of these strongmen overlap each other.

When Jesus asked the Gadarene demoniac spoken of in Luke 8 what his name was, he replied *"Legion,"* for there were many (Luke 8:30). These demons work together in order to have more power to destroy the person they inhabit or they are oppressing."

"But," you might say, "I'm not a liar." Have you (or do you) tell a person that you will meet them at a certain time and location and then don't show up on time but are late? If you are doing (or have done) this, then you are a liar, and your word is not good.

If we are truly children of the King, we cannot get away with this. If we are God's children, then He will correct, punish, or chasten us, as He promised in Hebrews 12:

> *If you endure chastening, God deals with you as with sons; for what son is there whom a father does not chasten? But if you are without chastening, of which all have become partakers, then you are illegitimate and not sons.*
>
> Hebrews 12:7-8

God loves us all and does not want any of us to perish, but rather, to become His children and live with Him forever. But we know that not all will be saved. This is very evident from the Word. Hell has enlarged itself for more victims of Satan's lies (see Isaiah 5:14). He is a liar and was from the beginning (see John 8:44). He is a thief, deceiver, a killer, and a destroyer, but Jesus came to give us life and life more abundantly (see John 10:10).

What is the punishment for this activity or life-style? Death, both physical and spiritual as we have seen in Revelation 21:8).

You shall destroy those who speak falsehood;
The LORD abhors the bloodthirsty and deceitful
man. Psalm 5:6

There are many other references in God's Word about liars and their sentence. We don't have space here to visit them all. You can see from what we have touched on that God hates the lies but loves the liar. He gave Himself for them to forgive and save them from Hell.

Always remember, when the devil comes to you with one of his lies, even after you have gone to the Lord for an answer to a situation or problem, that he is a liar, and there is no truth in him. When he does this, look up, for the answer is about to overtake you.

I have ministered to young people who have gotten caught up in Satan's lies and seen them wearing the yin and yang symbol, which is a circular disc, separated by a curved line across the disc. The top half is white and has a black dot in it, and the lower half is black with a white dot in it. I have explained to them that this represents black and white witchcraft, but they either don't believe it or think "there's a little good in all evil and a little evil in all good." How deceived can we and our children get? There is NO good in the devil, and there in NO evil in God.

Look at the word *devil*. What is the root of this word? "EVIL!" Satan is a LIAR. Period! This is why he will have eternal punishment in the Lake of Fire, as will all those who chose to follow him.

Hell was not created for human beings. It was created for Satan and his fallen angels. This was to be punishment for them alone. But, there are those who have chosen to believe Satan instead of believing the sincere Word of God. They will also have their part, there judgment, their punishment, with the devil, to be tormented by him for all eternity.

So, what do we do with this general or strong man?

FIRST: Cover yourself and anyone else present with the blood of Jesus for the divine protection of God. Find out if the person is a Christian. If not, lead them in the sinner's prayer, asking God to forgive their sins and asking Jesus into their lives as Lord and Savior.

SECOND: Bind the lying spirit and his cohorts (not the works of the flesh) in the name of Jesus and His blood. As you bind the strongman, stand strong in the authority given to you in Matthew 16:19, 18:18, and Mark 16:17. Jesus Himself has given us a promise that *"whatsoever [we] bind on earth SHALL be bound in heaven and whatsoever [we] loose on earth SHALL be loosed in heaven."* A more literal translation of this promise might read, *"Whatsoever you bind on earth is bound in the heavenlies, and whatsoever you loose on earth is also loosed in the heavenlies."* What is meant by "the heavenlies?" The realm above the earth where the devil and his angels operate.

Bind this strongman, and then you are able to "plunder" his house or place of residence, which is the person being ministered to, and take back everything he has held hostage or captive in the life of this person. In doing so, you are setting this person free in the name of Jesus.

THIRD: Loose the Spirit of Truth, which is the Holy Spirit of God, to lead them and guide them into all truth:

> *The Spirit of truth, whom the world [unsaved] cannot receive, because it neither sees Him nor knows Him; but you know Him, for He dwells with you and will be in you.* John 14:17

You have just bound the strongman in the name of Jesus, and you have loosed the Spirit of Truth to this individual and set them free to receive the healing and deliverance they so desperately needed. This is what *Spiritual Warfare and the Believer* is all about—using the weapons of war that God has given to us to set the captives free from the oppression and possession of the devil and his strongmen or generals.

> *Therefore take up the whole armor of God, that you may be able to withstand in the evil day, and having done all, to stand. Stand therefore, having girded your waist with truth, having put on the breastplate of righteousness, and having shod your feet with the preparation of the gospel of peace; above all, taking the shield of faith with which you will be able to quench all the fiery darts of the wicked one. And take the helmet of salvation, and the sword of the Spirit, which is the word of God; praying always with all prayer and supplication in the Spirit, being watchful to this end with all perseverance and supplication for all the saints.* Ephesians 6:13-18

We are the resident ranking officials of Heaven on this Earth, for we are filled with and endowed by the Holy Spirit, and it is our mission to do battle with the enemy for those whom he has taken captive. Use the authority of the believer to defeat the enemy in your life and that of your family and church. Be a disciple of Jesus Christ, and do what He would do, using the authority He has given you.

AUTHORITY: "Delegated power; the right to command; to enforce obedience; and to make final decisions over the works of the enemy."

— For Your Notes —

— FOR YOUR NOTES—

CHAPTER 5

PERVERSE SPIRIT

DEFINITION: *"To deviate from what is considered correct or acceptable; wickedness."* Strong's Concordance: *"to distort, to misinterpret, turn away, stubbornness."*

NOTE: The works of the flesh cannot be bound. They are free-will acts of the person, but they are controlled by demonic spirits that can and must be bound in order to set the person free. Again, Galatians 5:19-21 gives us a glimpse of these works of the flesh, which we can identify in the lives of persons who are being oppressed or possessed by the devil.

In Deuteronomy 18:9-14, God commanded the children of Israel NOT to learn to do the abominations of the inhabitants (heathen)[3] in these lands. It would be to

---

3. Definition of heathen: "a foreign nation or a troop of wild animals."

them death, He warned, yet they went against God's commands by learning and practiced heathen ways. The Law was given in Deuteronomy 17:14-20, and the Law was broken, as seen in 1 Kings 11: 1-11.

This general is known to all of us, and we see his activities in the lives of so many individuals. It is so prevalent in society that it is before our eyes every single day and is called "good." We can see the effects of it on TV, popular magazines, Facebook, and most any other social media outlet. Listed below are the manifestations or the "cohorts" of this general or strongman.

WOUNDED SPIRIT: To hit, cut, and mark, causing a scar (see Proverbs 15:4)

EVIL ACTIONS: Morally bad, wicked (see Psalm 78:36, Proverbs 17:20 and 23)

DOCTRINAL ERROR: Lying spirit, false teachers, a wrong belief, and a state of believing what is false or untrue (see Isaiah 19:14, Romans 1:22-23 and 2 Timothy 3:7-8)

CHRONIC WORRIER: Lasting a long time, recurring, acute (see Proverbs 19:13)

TWISTING THE WORD: To change the meaning (see Acts 13:10 and 2 Peter 2:14)

INCEST: Sexual relations between persons too closely related to marry legally (see 2 Samuel 13:2, 13 and 19 and Genesis 19:30-38)

CHILD ABUSE: To cause harm, mentally, physically, etc. to minors (see 2 Kings 23:10)

SEXUAL PERVERSIONS: Sodomy (sodomite, men) and homosexuality (catamite, women) (see Romans 1:17-32 and 2 Timothy 3:2)

CONTENTIOUS: Argumentative, quarrelsome (see Philippians 2:14-16, 1 Timothy 6:4-5 and Titus 3:10-11)

FOOLISH: Without good sense or wisdom (see Proverbs 1:22 and 19:1)

PORNOGRAPHY: Origination, a description of prostitutes and their trade, writings or pictures intended for sexual arousal (see 1 Kings 16:33, 18:19, 2 Kings 18:4 and 23:14)

FILTHY MIND: Having unclean and uncontrolled thoughts (see Proverbs 2:12 and 23:33)

ABORTION: Medically induced procedure of premature birth of a child ending in death (see Proverbs 6:17, Joel 3:19, 2 Kings 23:10, Leviticus 18:21 and Deuteronomy 12:31)

ATHEIST: A belief that there is no God (see Proverbs 14:2, Psalm 14:1 and Romans 1:30)

As you can see, there are a large number of works of the flesh (or cohorts) identified with this strongman. Just as God warned Moses and the children of Israel, as they were entering the Promised Land, not to learn to do after the abominations of the inhabitants of the land, not to learn their practices nor engage in them and to do so was death, He is also warning us today not to learn or engage in this sort of lifestyle. Why? Because to us, it is also death (both physical and spiritual). Yet, we see so many learning from the Hollywood crowd and accepting that their form of perversion as "normal." The devil is still a liar.

These things are against the Lord God that we serve. To Him they are abominations. They are sickening to Him, vulgar and dirty. In Matthew 17:17, Jesus called *"faithless and perverse,"* those, whether individuals or nations, that would involve themselves in this way of living and under the control of this strongman.

The apostle Paul said to young Timothy, in 1 Timothy 6:1-5, that those who did these things were carnally minded and that lived by the carnal mind would experience death. According to Paul, *"The just [the Christian] SHALL live by faith"* (Romans 1:17), faith in our Lord and Savior Jesus Christ, not by the carnal mind and senses. If this is the wish of our heavenly Father, then why are so many Christians getting involved in a debased lifestyle? Why do we yield our minds and bodies to this demon of Satan?

The Word tells us that this desire is already inside of our soul (mind, will, and emotions). Therefore, if we have not renewed our minds with the washing of the water of the Word of God, bound this strongman, and caused him to submit to the will of the Father, it is easy for him to exert his will over our bodies. From there comes death—both physical and spiritual.

Every human being on the face of the earth is under attack from the host of fallen angelic beings under Satan's control, but Jesus has given back to us the authority Adam lost in the Garden of Eden. When

Jesus rose from the grave, He told the disciples (both then and now), that ALL POWER had been given back to Him both in Heaven and Earth, and He continued, "GO YE, THEREFORE" (Matthew 28:19). Jesus returned to the Church what Adam had lost in the garden through the seduction of Eve and his subsequent rebellion against the command of God not to eat of the fruit of the tree in the middle of the garden.

If all power has been given back to us, then why are we not walking in that authority and subduing the enemy? Is it because of fear? Is it because of a lack of knowledge of the Word and of the authority of every believer? It's all of the above. Mainly, it's because the Body of Christ (the Church) has not been taught, nor have we submersed ourselves in the river of life, THE WORD, and learned it well enough.

When Janice and I started this walk in deliverance in December of 1979, we knew absolutely nothing about deliverance or authority. All we knew was that we had been prophesied to about this new ministry and phase in our lives. We were anointed by a very precious Holy Ghost-Filled, completed Jewish woman who had survived the Nazi Auschwitz Death Camp. The Holy Ghost instructed us to read the four gospels and to pay strict attention to what Jesus said and did. Then we could do the same things He had done, because the power that raised Him from the dead was in us, to empower us to do those things too. We were to speak what we heard Jesus speak and do what we saw Jesus do. If we were obedient to simply do those things, our ministry would be successful.

Our first deliverance session was barely four months later, and we totally depended on the Holy Ghost to guide us through it. It was a complete success. We have continued in that ministry for more than forty years now. I have since earned my Ph.D. in Biblical Studies to further aid in this ministry and for more understanding of God and His Word. We have been obedient and successful, and are still totally dependent on the Holy Spirit.

So, what do we do to take care of this strongman?

FIRST: We cover everyone present (including ourselves) with the blood of Jesus for divine protection from this strongman entering us or them. We ask if the person is a Christian. If not, we lead them in the prayer of salvation asking God to forgive them of their sins, and asking Jesus to come into their lives as their Lord and Savior.

SECOND: We bind the perverse spirit in the name of Jesus, according to Matthew 16:19 and 18:18 and

Mark 16:17 and 23-24 and use the authority given us in Luke 10:19 to send this demon and its cohorts back to the pits they came from. We command the spirit to never return in Jesus' name, according to Mark 9:25.

THIRD: We loose the Holy Spirit to bring the Spirit of grace and supplication, according to Zechariah 12:10 and Hebrews 10:29. The definition of *grace* is: "kindness, favor, divine influence upon the heart. Supplication: earnest prayer or bestowed favor."

The roots of this general are rooted in the flesh and are seen as *"works of the flesh"* (Galatians 5: 19-21). How do we know them? Matthew 7:20 states:

By their fruits you [SHALL] know them.
(Emphasis Mine)

Remember, You have been given back the authority Adam lost in the garden. The definition of that authority is:

"Delegated power, the right to command, to enforce obedience, to make final decisions regarding the enemy's activity in your life or that of your family or church."

— FOR YOUR NOTES —

— FOR YOUR NOTES—

CHAPTER 6

SPIRIT OF HAUGHTINESS

DEFINITION: *"Proud and vain to the point of arrogance, excessively and unpleasant self-importance, insolent, overbearing and proud."*

NOTE: The works of the flesh cannot be bound. They are free-will acts of the person, but they are controlled by demonic spirits that can and must be bound in order to set the person free. Again, Galatians 5:19-21 gives us a glimpse of these works of the flesh that we can identify in the life of persons being oppressed or possessed by the devil.

In Deuteronomy 18:9-14, God commanded the children of Israel NOT to learn to do after the abominations of the inhabitants (heathen[4]) in the lands they would subdue. It would be to them death. Yet they went against God's commands and learned and practiced these

4. Definition of *heathen*: "a foreign nation or a troop of animals"

abominations. The Law was given in Deuteronomy 17:14-20, and the Law was broken, as seen in 1 Kings 11:1-11.

This general is also known to all of us. We see his ugly head in many places and faces, and it is the same—that smug, arrogant look that says, "Why are you breathing my air? I'm so superior to you, and you just need to go away."

Do you recognize this demon or strongman? I know you do. Why? Because every one of us has one in our family, circle of friends, or church. "Church?" you may ask? Yes. They're sitting in the church, and some are sitting next to you. Every church has its very own clique, and the haughty spirit is the controller of the group.

Listed below are the signs, manifestations (or cohorts) of this general (or strongman). I want to remind you that some of the generals, or strongmen, overlap with others, and such is the case with this general, spirit of haughtiness.

PRIDE: Having too high an opinion of oneself, conceit, arrogance (see Proverbs 6:16-17, 16:18-19, 28:25 and Isaiah 16:6)

OBSTINATE: Tenaciously unwilling to yield, difficult to control or manage (see Proverbs 29:1 and Daniel 5:20)

100

REBELLION: An open act or show of defiance toward authority (see 1 Samuel 15:23 and Proverbs 29:1).[5]

SELF-RIGHTEOUSNESS: Smugly sure of one's own righteousness (good works) (see Luke 18:11-12)

SELF-DECEPTION: To deceive oneself, to refuse truth (see Jeremiah 49:16, Obadiah 1:3 and Matthew 7:4).[6]

CONTENTIOUS: Given to contention, quarrelsome, belligerent (see Proverbs 18:6, 1 Corinthians 11:16 and Galatians 5:20)

IDLENESS: Laziness, inactive (sluggard) (see Ezekiel 16:49-50, Proverbs 6:6-11, 13:14 and 15:19)

STRIFE: Bitter, often violent, dissention or conflict (see Proverbs 28:25).[7]

REJECTION OF GOD: Rejecting the Word of

---

5. This overlaps with the spirit of divination
6. This overlaps with the lying spirit
7. This overlaps with the spirit of jealousy

God and/or the prophet of God (see Jeremiah 43:2 and Hosea 4:6).[8]

SCORNFUL: Contempt or disdain, to consider or treat as contemptible or despicable (see Proverbs 1:22, 3:34, 21:24 and 29:8)

ARROGANT-SMUG: Self-satisfied or complacent ("I did it MY way.:) (see 2 Samuel 22:28, Jeremiah 48:29, Isaiah 2:11 and 17:5:15)

As you can see, this spirit is also a very dangerous general. He is and will be responsible for the destruction of many souls in the Lake of Fire, Hell, because he leads many into thinking they are good enough through good works and education and don't need Jesus Christ as their Savior. We see this general in many of the modern cults that teach another gospel. Good works, they believe, will get them into Heaven.

This general, as seen in the manifestations, or cohorts, is linked to the lying spirit. In Galatians 5:19-21 and 1 Samuel 15:23, this is classified as the same spirit as witchcraft (rebellion). The apostle Paul said, in Galatians 5:19-21, that those who practice these things *"SHALL NOT inherit the kingdom of God."*

8. This overlaps with the lying spirit

Again, what does that little seemingly-insignificant word *shall* mean? It is a legal term that means "mandatory obligation to be completed or fulfilled." When we see it in the Word of God, especially spoken by Jesus, He is putting all of Heaven under mandatory obligation to see to it that our request or prayer is fulfilled. Neither Heaven, nor God, Jesus nor the Holy Spirit are liars, and therefore God's Word SHALL be fulfilled.

As you read Galatians 5:19-21, you will see that these are manifestations of the strongman and are called *"works of the flesh,"* which are dead works apart from the Holy Ghost and salvation.

What is the ultimate punishment for this sin if not confessed and repented of? DEATH! Again, Galatians 5:21 says very clearly, *"Those who practice these things SHALL NOT inherit the Kingdom of God."*

That word *inherit* means "to be an heir, a sharer or possessor of something." The person living this lifestyle and demonstrating these manifestations cannot be an heir to the things God has laid up for His children. Romans 6:23 tells us that *"the wages of sin is death, but the gift of God is eternal life in Christ Jesus."* We have this choice to make in order to inherit the gifts of the Father.

King Solomon tells us, in Proverbs 16:18, that this spirit leads to death and destruction in Hell for eternity.

What are the requirements God has placed into action for us to live a life pleasing to Him? How do we gain access into the presence of God? What allows us to keep coming back into His presence? The prophet Micah gives us these requirements in Micah 6:8:

> *He has shown you, O man, what is good;*
> *And what does the LORD require of you,*
> *But to do justly,*
> *To love mercy,*
> *And to walk humbly with your God.*

These requirements are very straightforward and clear. If we do these things, we will be accepted into the presence of God and not rejected for our haughty attitude. How, then, do we deal with this general or strongman?

FIRST: We cover everyone present (including ourselves) with the blood of Jesus to prevent this spirit from entering any other person. We ask if this person is a Christian. If not, lead them in the prayer of salvation, asking God to forgive them of their sins, and asking Jesus to come into their lives as Lord and Savior.

SECOND: We bind the spirit of haughtiness in the name of Jesus and command it to leave with its cohorts and never return to the person ever again, as seen in Matthew 16:19 and 18:18.

We also see a precedence for commanding the unclean spirit to never return in Mark 9:25, where a young man would often throw himself into the fire or water to kill himself. As the crowd was running toward Jesus to see what was happening, He bound the spirit and commanded it: *"Come out of him and enter him no more"* (Mark 9:25).

This is one of the things many ministers fail to do. They forget the example Jesus gave us when dealing with the deliverance of a person, and they leave the door open for the unclean spirit or spirits to return by not taking this authority and commanding the spirit or the spirits to never return. That leaves the person vulnerable to further attack.

We must remember that Jesus is the example for us to follow. He gave us the formula for success, and if we follow that formula, we SHALL be successful. One good example is this: Every cook has a cookbook with their favorite recipes for their favorite dishes. If you follow the recipe, that cake, gumbo, pie, or whatever you are cooking will come out as it should. But if you fail to follow the recipe to the letter, there is a great chance the food will not be edible or it will taste different than expected. Until you have the recipe saved to memory, continue to look at the book for instructions. Once that recipe is firm in your mind, you can then eliminate that part of the cooking process and still be successful. Do the same with God's Word.

THIRD: We loose the Holy Spirit, a humble and contrite Spirit, according to Proverbs 16:19 and Romans 1:4. If we fail to loose the Holy Spirit as being the needed replacement, the person will be in danger of worse consequences. The Word tells us in Matthew 12:43-45:

> *When an unclean spirit goes out of a man, he goes through dry places, seeking rest, and finds none. Then he says, "I will return to my house from which I came." And when he comes, he finds it empty, swept, and [garnished]. Then he goes and takes with him seven other spirits more wicked than himself, and they enter and dwell there; and the last state of that man is worse than the first.*

This is why it is so vitally important to allow the Holy Spirit to bring the needed replacement.

This phrase, *"swept and garnished,"* literally means "religiously decorated." The house looks good from the outside, but there is nothing inside but dead works.

Deliverance is a very serious thing. If we fail to follow the recipe given to us by Jesus, it could end in disaster. If the person you are about to minister deliverance to does not or is not ready for this process, DO NOT put your hands on them and pray for them! You will only be adding misery to misery and trouble to trouble. Why? Because their sufferings will be seven times worse than at the beginning. Janice and I have seen this happen, and it's not a pretty sight or a good feeling.

Ask that person if they're ready to be free from the unclean spirit that has them bound or is harassing them. If they say, "Yes," then proceed with the ministry to that person. If they say, "No," then back off until they're ready. Sometimes they need more time with the frogs.

How will you recognize this spirit? Matthew 7:20 says, *"By their fruits you [shall] know them."* Watch how they are acting and what they are saying. Out of the abundance of the heart, the mouth speaks.

What is in the heart of the individual will come out of their mouth—righteousness or unrighteousness (see Luke 6:45).

And remember, you are a child of the King and have been given authority over the works of the enemy.

AUTHORITY: "Delegated power, the right to enforce obedience, to make final decisions regarding the enemy's activity in your life, family, church, or another person. "

— For Your Notes —

— FOR YOUR NOTES—

CHAPTER 7

SPIRIT OF HEAVINESS

DEFINITION: *"Having great weight, intense or sustained to a great or excessive degree, a villain, grievous sadness* [see Romans 9:2 and 5], *to cause grief, to be in heaviness, to be sorrowful* [see 1 Peter 1:6]"

NOTE: The works of the flesh cannot be bound. They are free-will acts of the person, but they are controlled by demonic spirits that can and must be bound in order to set the person free. Again, Galatians 5:19-21 gives us a glimpse of these works of the flesh that we can identify in the life of persons being oppressed or possessed by the devil

In Deuteronomy 18:9-14, God commanded the children of Israel NOT to learn to do after the abominations of the inhabitants (heathen[9]) in the lands

9. Definition of *heathen:* "A foreign nation or a troop of animals."

they would conquer. It would be to them death. Still, they went against God's commands and learned and practiced the heathen ways. The Law was given in Deuteronomy 17: 14-20, and the Law was broken, as seen in 1 Kings 11:1-11.

This general, or strongman, is a very vicious being. He comes on the scene when there is a traumatic event in the life of an individual, such as the death of a loved one, friend, or spouse, or a divorce, the loss of a job, or any other such traumatic event. This strongman is relentless in his pursuit and attempts to control or bring death to an individual, as seen by the manifestations or the cohorts exhibited by him. Listed below are some of the visible signs to look for.

EXCESSIVE MOURNING: An expression of excessive grief (see Isaiah 61:3, Psalm 38:6, Jeremiah 31:13 and Luke 4:18)

SORROW-GRIEF: Mental suffering because of loss, deep sadness over loss (see Nehemiah 2:2, Isaiah 53:3-4 and Proverbs 15:13)

BROKEN HEARTED: Overwhelmed by grief or despair (see Psalm 69:20, Luke 4:18, Proverbs 12:18, 15:3, 13 and 18:14)

SUICIDAL TENDENCIES, THOUGHTS, AND SUICIDE: Self murder (see Mark 9:14-29)

INNER HURTS, TORN SPIRIT: To offend, damage, cause mental sufferings (see Luke 4:18, Proverbs 18:14, 22 and 26:22)

HEAVINESS: Having great mental or spiritual weight (see Isaiah 61:3)

SELF-PITY: Excessive pity for oneself (see Psalm 69:20)

REJECTION: Unaccepted, thrown out, to be shoved aside (see Hosea 4:6, Luke 17:22-26 and Isaiah 53:3-4)

DEPRESSION: A mental condition of gloom, sadness, or dejection (see Isaiah 61:3)

DESPAIR, DEJECTION, HOPELESSNESS: A total lack of any hope (see 2 Corinthians 1:8-9)

INSOMNIA; INABILITY TO SLEEP: (see Nehemiah 2:2)

MANIC DEPRESSION: May include episodes of low energy, low motivation, loss of interest in daily activities and may last for days to months and be associated with suicidal thoughts (see Mark 9:14-29)

NOTE: We can also add to this list of cohorts: alcohol and drug use, eating disorders (gluttony) and any other substance used to self-medicate the person to make them feel better.

I have seen more of this general, or strongman, in operation in the more than forty years of ministry in deliverance than any other. But, as I've said in previous texts, these twelve generals or strongmen very often overlap, giving more power or resistance from other evil generals to the Gospel of Jesus Christ.

Something more than thirty years ago I dealt with this general in my own life. I felt first-hand the dark pit of despair, grief, and loneliness one feels dropped into. This grief and loneliness seemed more than a human could bear. The feeling of betrayal and rejection were so real it was almost unbearable. This is when or where the thought of suicide comes into the picture. If I said I didn't think of that, I would be lying. Everyone who deals with this spirit at one time or another has these thoughts and feelings.

Because of the grief and mental state of mind, we sometimes begin to withdraw inside of ourselves in an effort to hide from the pain, and we can't think of anything but the loneliness, separation, and rejection, even forgetting to eat or drink to help keep the body going. You go to work, but you are in a fog of despair, not caring about anything but your pain. That is where the temptation to use alcohol, drugs, and/or other stimulants enter to help ease the pain and give you the energy to move forward.

In my case, I never submitted to the use of any drugs or alcohol. I had enough of the Word of God in my spirit and heart that it prevented me from doing so. It was during this time in my life when I learned more about intercession and the authority that has been given to us as children of God. I had been to Bible college and taken courses in "the Authority of the Believer," "Spiritual Warfare," "Intercessory Prayer," and many other subjects, but it was only after I was placed in God's School of Higher Learning and started putting into practice what was in my head that things began to change. Was it just head knowledge or was it in my heart? Over the coming years, I was about to find out.

As I began to do spiritual warfare over my life and my family, I came to understand just how much God loves us, and I started to stand up to the devil and his demonic strongmen. I read all I could find on this subject from godly men whom I trusted and who had been through the fire of sanctification, as I was going through. These were men like Dr. Kenneth Hagen, Dr. Oral Roberts, Pastor Kenneth Copeland, Pastor Rebecca Brown, and Pastor Mary K. Baxter, just to name a few.

With these men and women encouraging me, and the wisdom and knowledge the Holy Spirit was giving me, I survived the test by fire. This is why I can say to you today that God's Word is stronger and more powerful than any situation or circumstance you will ever encounter in your entire life.

I said all of that to say that we can have the breakthrough we and others need in Jesus Christ. He has equipped us with the necessary tools needed to set the captives free, and this includes setting ourselves free. The Holy Spirit has given us a mandate to go to the world and preach the Gospel to every creature, taking the good news that Jesus Christ is on the throne of Heaven and making intercession for us.

We are to minister to the whole man—spirit, soul, and body. How are we to do this and take back what this general or strongman has stolen from us, our family and church?

FIRST: We cover everyone (including ourselves) with the blood of Jesus to prevent this demon from entering someone else. We must remember the compassion Jesus had for the sick and oppressed and minister to them in that manner. The Word tells us, *"He was moved with compassion for them, and healed their sick"* (Matthew 14:14). The key here is the word *compassion*. Because Jesus had compassion, the Holy Spirit was able to freely move in and through Him to complete the task before Him.

We ask if the person is a Christian. If not, we lead them in a prayer of salvation and ask Jesus for forgiveness of their sins.

SECOND: We bind this demonic general of heaviness in the name of Jesus and send it back to his place in the pit. Then, according to Mark 9:25, we command this general and his cohorts to never return to this person again in Jesus' name.

Remember that many of the people we minister to in deliverance have suffered tremendous blows to their spiritual being as well as their bodies. They are hurt, wounded, and bruised—spiritually, physically, and emotionally—and need the love of Jesus Christ and the strength of the Holy Spirit to help them through the ordeal they are or were in.

These people need to be reminded of Isaiah 53:3-5 and what Jesus went through for our salvation and of Hebrews 4:12-15, which shows us that He feels our infirmities. Why? Because He was God in human form and knows what a human being feels on a daily basis.

THIRD: We loose the power and anointing of the Holy Spirit to the person for comfort, the garment of praise, and the oil of gladness and joy found in Romans 5:1-5, John 15:25, and Isaiah 61:3. This is the only way to minister to and bring healing to the person dealing with this general. You cannot medicate them and expect good results. Why? Because when it's all said and done, all you have is a medicated human with the same demonic stronghold in their life. This demon must be dealt with, for it is the root of the problem. Dealing only with the superficial manifestations of the strongman will accomplish very little.

Again, how will you recognize this spirit? Matthew 7:20 says, *"By their fruits you [shall] know them."*

118

Watch how they are acting and what they are saying. Out of the abundance of the heart the mouth speaks (see Matthew 12:34). What is in the heart of the individual will come out of their mouth—righteousness or unrighteousness (see Luke 6:45).

Remember, you are a child of the King and have been given authority over the works of the enemy. Use the authority that has been delegated to you for the Kingdom of God.

AUTHORITY: "Delegated power, the right to enforce obedience, to make final decisions regarding the enemy's activity in your life, family, church or another person."

— For Your Notes—

CHAPTER 8

SPIRIT OF WHOREDOMS

DEFINITION: *"Prostitution, to offer one's body for sexual acts in exchange for monetary gain, to devote one's talents to an unworthy cause, to commit adultery or idolatry, either physically or spiritually."*

NOTE: The works of the flesh cannot be bound. They are free-will acts of the person, but they are controlled by demonic spirits that can and must be bound in order to set the person free. Again, Galatians 5:19-21 gives us a glimpse of these works of the flesh that we can identify in the life of persons being oppressed or possessed by the devil.

In Deuteronomy 18:9-14, God commanded the children of Israel NOT to learn to do after the abominations of the inhabitants (heathen[10]) in the lands

---

10. An irreligious, uncivilized, unenlightened person. One who adheres to a religion that does not acknowledge the Lord of Judaism or Christianity.

they would inhabit. It would be to them death. Still, they went against God's commands and learned and practiced these abominations.

The Law was given in Deuteronomy 17:14-20, and the Law was broken, as seen in 1 Kings 11:1-11. Why have I added this note and warning to each chapter as I was writing this? Because I believe it is necessary to get the point across to every reader, so they will understand that this is no game. You need to understand the implications involved. I don't want anyone of you to wind up like the seven sons of Sceva, as recorded in Acts 19:14-16. Just because these men were the sons of the High Priest did not guarantee that they could perform deliverance on a needy man. They were not equipped spiritually to do the job, and it cost them dearly.

I don't want this same outcome to happen to those of you who are reading this book. The cohorts of some of these generals or strongmen are deadly, and for this reason you must know how and what you are dealing with. Below is a list of those cohorts:

UNFAITHFULNESS-ADULTERY: Sexual intercourse between a married person and one other than the lawful spouse (see Ezekiel 16:15, 28, Proverbs 5:1-14 and Galatians 5:19-21)[11]

11. This also includes adultery of the heart.

122

PROSTITUTION: 1) To offer one's body for sexual acts in exchange for monetary gain, to devote ones talents to an unworthy cause; 2) To commit adultery or idolatry; either physically or spiritually (see Ezekiel 16:15, 28, Proverbs 5:1-14 and 7:23)

LOVE OF MONEY: Greed, lust (see Proverbs 15:27 and 1 Timothy 6:7-14)

IDOLATRY: To worship idols; blind admiration or devotion (see Judges 2:17 and Ezekiel 16)[12]

WORLDLINESS: Devoted to the concerns of the world rather than spiritual matters (see James 4:1-11, especially verse 4)

FORNICATION: Sexual relations between persons not married to each other (see Hosea 4:13-19 and Deuteronomy 23:17-18)

EXCESSIVE APPETITE: Going beyond what is usual, necessary, proper, or normal (gluttony, greed) (see 1 Corinthians 6:13-16 and 3:17-20, especially verse 19))

---

12. All the strongmen of the lying spirit overlap with slander and gossip.

CHRONIC DISSATISFACTION: Of long duration, without end, continuing, lingering (see Ezekiel 16:28)

We can see this strongman in operation in the Word of God in Galatian 5:19-21, 1 Corinthians 6:9-10, and Romans 1:21-23. We can also see a very good example of its works in the book of Hosea.

The prophet Hosea was instructed by God to marry a prostitute as an example to the children of Israel of their relationship with God. Hosea was reluctant to do this, but he was finally obedient to God's wishes.

The woman Hosea married had borne three illegitimate children because of her many infidelities. Ultimately, she had been sold into slavery and then Hosea redeemed her, bought her back by paying the required price for her salvation from that lifestyle of whoredoms.

Today, so many are caught up in this ungodly lifestyle and think it's fun. What they don't realize is what a terrible price they will eventually pay, what terrible consequences will result—broken relationships, diseases that medical science has no cure for, other strongmen entering the picture (the spirit of heaviness and the spirit of sickness), fear, bondage to the lifestyle, drugs, and eventually DEATH.

This death is both physical and spiritual, unless the person repents and is delivered by the power of the Holy Spirit, the Word of God, and the blood of Jesus Christ.

"But," you may ask, "what does this have to do with me?" We are the children of the Most High God and are called to the ministry of reconciliation, and also to use the authority given to us to set the captives free from this and other strongmen. We are ambassadors of the Kingdom of God here on Earth. When an ambassador of any country is sent to another country, that person represents the government and it interests in that foreign country. That ambassador is empowered to make decisions pertaining to the wellbeing and interests of his native country.

We are citizens of the Kingdom of Heaven and have been empowered by our Master, our Lord and Savior and God, to make final decisions on this Earth pertaining to the Kingdom we represent. This includes the authority over any demonic being who is trying to kill, steal, or destroy a citizen of Heaven. We have also been given the ministry of reconciliation of friendship and fellowship between God and man, others, and one another.

125

So what do we do in the battle for the soul of people entangled with and by this strongman?

FIRST: We cover everyone present (including ourselves) with the blood of Jesus for their protection so that this demonic being does not enter others. We must then identify the area of ministry needed. How do we do that? By taking a moment and praying in the Holy Spirit for His guidance and wisdom. He will show you the areas that need to be addressed, how to handle it, and what to bind in the person's life.

There have been many occasions in which I was ministering to a person or group of persons, and the Holy Spirit would give me a word of knowledge regarding a person or persons in that group. It's the same with a single individual to be ministered to. What is so very important is to always stay plugged-in or tuned into the Holy Spirit for His guidance. That way you don't need to spend a long time in prayer to have His wisdom.

So, this is necessary, but you might ask, "How do we do that?" The Word says for us to always be in prayer or a state or attitude of prayer. By keeping the altar of our hearts clean and free of the sin and cares of the world, we can walk in the Spirit of God.

This allows the Holy Spirit to constantly be in communication with your spirit.

After we have received instructions from the Holy Spirit, we then ask if this person is a Christian or not. If they are not, then we lead them in the sinner's prayer, asking God for forgiveness of their sin and asking Jesus to come into their lives as Lord and Savior.

SECOND: The second thing to do is bind the spirit of whoredoms and his cohorts, send them back to the pit, and command them to never return to the person again in the name of Jesus. You bind the spirit, not the works of the flesh or cohorts, according to Matthew 18:18.

Sometimes these spirits don't want to leave their house, and they will scream, fight, spit, curse, or do other things to make you stop. They are comfortable there in their nest. On many occasions, while in a deliverance session, I have witnessed these unclean spirits making the person fall to the floor or ground, and they will cause that person to slither on their back or belly like a snake. Many times the person will begin to vomit a green slime, which is the nest or home of the demonic spirit that they have set up in the person.

Coughing, sneezing, yawning, burping, and passing gas are just a few examples of manifestations to look for that will indicate that the unclean spirits are leaving the human body. Sometimes there is no reaction, but there usually are.

THIRD: We loose the power of the Holy Spirit to bring to that person the Spirit of God's pure and righteous Spirit, to fill that void left by the strongman being evicted from his home. If the person is willing, it is a very good idea to then lead them into the baptism of the Holy Spirit. If not, then pray over them for the Holy Spirit to take up residence in them and give them the power to resist the unclean spirit.

Again, how will you recognize this spirit? Matthew 7:20 says, *"By their fruits you [shall] know them."* Watch how they are acting and what they are saying. Out of the abundance of the heart, the mouth speaks. What is in the heart of the individual will come out of their mouth—righteousness or unrighteousness (see Luke 6:45).

Many times I have smelled the demon involved in a person's life. Some have the smell of a sick stomach; some have the smell of smoke or fire from Hell. Have all of your spiritual senses operating so that you can discern what is happening.

Remember, you are an ambassador of the Kingdom of God, and you have been empowered by the Holy Spirit with authority over the enemy.

AUTHORITY: "The right to command, to enforce obedience, to make final decisions over the enemies' activities in your life, your family's life, the church, and those who come for you to minister deliverance in their lives."

— For Your Notes—

SPIRIT OF BONDAGE

DEFINITION: *"The condition of a slave or serf, slavery or servitude, to serve, till, work, enslave."*

NOTE: The works of the flesh cannot be bound. They are free-will acts of the person, but they are controlled by demonic spirits that can and must be bound in order to set the person free. Again, Galatians 5:19-21 gives us a glimpse of these works of the flesh that we can identify in the life of persons being oppressed or possessed by the devil.

What are the cohorts associated with this general or strongman?

FEAR: A feeling of alarm, a state of dread (see Romans 8:15, 2 Timothy 1:7, 1 John 4:18, Revelation 21:8, and 22:15)[13]

---

13. Overlaps with the spirit of fear

FEAR OF DEATH: A state of dread (see Hebrews 2:14-15)[14]

ADDICTIONS: To give or devote oneself habitually or compulsively (drugs, alcohol, tobacco, etc.) (see Romans 8:15 and 2 Peter 2:19)

COMPULSIVE SIN: A strong impulse to act; being compelled or forced (see Proverbs 5:22 and John 8:34)

SERVANT OF CORRUPTION: One employed to perform immoral, depraved, or dishonest actions (see Romans 6:16, 7:23, Luke 8:26-29, Acts 8:23, John 8:34 and 2 Peter 2:19)

BONDAGE TO SIN: The condition of a slave, servitude, slavery (see 2 Timothy 2:26)

CAPTIVE OF SATAN: A prisoner, one who is enslaved by a strong emotion, under restraints or control (see 2 Peter 2:19 and 2 Timothy 2:26)

As stated earlier in the book, some of these strongmen overlap with each other to add resistance to the Word of God in a person's life. This adds strength to

14. Also overlaps with the spirit of fear

the demonic force inhabiting the person, preventing them from being set free from their stronghold. We saw this in Chapter 7, the spirit of heaviness and his cohorts. In that group of manifestations, we saw the introduction of drugs, alcohol, and other stimulants. This general takes advantage of the use of these products and puts an overwhelming desire for the taste and feel of them in the human body, resulting in what the world calls "addiction." We know him by the name "spirit of bondage."

This general has set up housekeeping and has absolutely no intention of leaving his home. Remember the Gadarene man in Luke 8:26-29) who was demon possessed? When Jesus asked the demon his name, he answered, *"Legion, for we are many"* (Mark 5:9).

When Jesus commanded the demons to leave the man, the demons cried and asked Jesus to allow them to enter into the bodies of a herd of hogs. Why hogs? Because the demons need an earthly body to possess as a home away from their real home–Hell. Jesus granted them permission to enter the hogs, and the animals could not tolerate their bodies being inhabited by demons. It drove them crazy, and they ran down a cliff into the Sea of Galilee and were killed.

Our bodies are a perfect habitation for evil spirits. Our make-up, physically and spiritually, is an ideal place for them to live. We can tolerate their being in us, at least for a season. When they begin to multiply is when the real dangers come. They begin to affect our health and mental stability, to the point that they need removing.

Humans, however, were not designed to house these unclean inhabitants. We were designed for only one spirit to dwell in us, and that is the Holy Spirit of God. The Holy Spirit brings us the peace, love, and joy of our Lord. Demonic spirits bring us chaos, hatred, and death—spiritual, physical, and eternal.

The apostle Paul wrote in Romans 6:16:

Do you not know that to whom you present yourselves slaves to obey, you are that one's slaves whom you obey, whether of sin leading to death, or of obedience leading to righteousness?

Why do I call this a spirit of bandage? Because you are bound to that strongman or demonic force. We cannot say, "The devil made me do it." Why? Because you and I have a condition in us from birth called "the sin nature." It was inherited from our former fallen father, Adam.

It's already in our souls to allow the devil to entice us and lead us away from the truths of God. So, when that carrot is dangled in front of us, we simple go after it. When we are tempted and yield to the temptation, then sin enters. When we submit to the sin, death enters. We become bound by the sin, and in many cases we enjoy it (at least for a season). This is what the apostle Paul was trying to convey to us. When we yield to a temptation, we become entangled and bound to that sin.

This bondage can be to anything that controls us, such as alcohol, drugs, food, sex, tobacco, money ... and the list goes on. Many of these come from the spirit of heaviness. Why? Because of some traumatic event in our lives. We are trying to deal with the pain that is associated with the heaviness or emptiness in our lives. So, we self-medicate.

This is found in every family to some extent. I have seen it in my family, but, thank God for His faithfulness. Those members were delivered and now live normal, productive lives, contributing to society as healthy citizens.

For far too many—untold millions—this spirit of bondage enslaves the unsuspecting and keeps them longer than they want to stay. It takes them farther than they want to go, and it makes them pay more than they are willing to pay. Too often, the price is life itself.

In many cases, this bondage starts even before we are born. Many times, even while in the womb, we make inner vows from an event that has happened to us. Before I was ever born, I made such a vow. My biological father had deserted my mother and me and took up with another woman. He wrote a letter to my mother, telling her he didn't want her anymore nor the baby she was carrying. I heard, in the womb, my grandmother reading this letter out loud to my mother, and as I heard those words, I made a vow: "I would never allow a man to get close to me and be my friend."

Some forty years later, I confronted my mother about those words that I had heard, and she started to weep and told me the story. At that point, I realized why I had no male friends and repented of the vow, confessed it as sin, and asked God to forgive me.

When I confessed, the vow was broken. That day I felt a lifting of oppression in my spirit and knew that it was done. From that point on, I started allowing men into my life, and now I have a host of men I can call friends.

I was in bondage to this strongman by something I had done even before I was born, and there are many who are suffering from the same thing. There, again, is where we can see the overlapping of the spirit of heaviness and inner hurts, torn spirits, and rejections entering into play.

So, how do we deal with this general or strongman?

FIRST: We cover everyone present (including ourselves) with the blood of Jesus for protection and to prevent this general from entering into anyone else. We must identify the areas needed to set the person free from this general, and we do so by taking a moment to pray in the Spirit to get His direction, wisdom, and understanding. This person needs to be ministered to in every aspect of their lives.

We also need to determine if the person is a Christian. If not, we then lead them in the sinner's prayer, asking God for forgiveness of their sins and asking Jesus into their lives as Lord and Savior.

The whole man or person needs healing. Why? Because this bondage has affected their whole being. We must get to the root of the bondage. I have ministered to many people in this area, and many times I have had the Holy Spirit tell me to take that person back into their childhood, even before they were born, and tell me what happened. When we begin to identify the source of the bondage, their face begins to light up, and their countenance changes from one of despair to one of hope.

Deal with the inner vows and hurts, the rejections, and any other source of the bondage.

SECOND: Bind this general or strongman and his cohorts in the name of Jesus and command him back to his place in the pit, and also command him to never return to this person, according to Mark 9:25.

Remember, that evil spirit is going to wander the dry places, seeking rest for a season. When he finds no rest, because he has been evicted from his home, he will return to see the condition of that house. If he finds it swept and garnished, he will go and find seven others more evil than himself and return to his house, and the end result of that person will be worse than the beginning.

If the person agrees, then lead them into the baptism, or infilling, of the Holy Spirit in their life. Why the infilling of the Holy Spirit? The phrase *"swept and garnished"* means "religiously decorated," but there is nothing there except a good appearance. By having that person filled with the presence and Person of the Holy Spirit, there is then no room for that demon to return to the house. It is occupied by the power of God.

THIRD: Loose the Holy Spirit and His presence, with the Spirit of liberty in Christ Jesus and the Spirit of adoption, also found in Romans 8:15. There the apostle Paul said:

> *For you did not receive the spirit of bondage again to fear, but you received the Spirit of adoption by whom we cry out, "Abba, Father [DADDY GOD]!"*

You may be saying, "I can't do that." Yes, you can. Our Father has empowered you to do this and even greater things. The Word of God says so. Jesus Himself said it in John 14:12. Read it for yourselves, and see if it's not true.

Remember the word *shall*. If Jesus said it, then all of Heaven is under mandatory obligation that what you have spoken would come to pass when it lines up with the will of the Father and heart of the throne. You have the authority of Heaven.

AUTHORITY: "Delegated power, the right to command, to enforce obedience, to make final decisions regarding the devil's activity in your life, that of your family, church and in this earth."

139

— FOR YOUR NOTES—

CHAPTER 10

SPIRIT OF FEAR

DEFINITION: *"A feeling of alarm or dread."*

NOTE: The works of the flesh cannot be bound. They are free-will acts of the person, but they are controlled by demonic spirits that can and must be bound in order to set the person free. Again, Galatians 5:19-21 gives us a glimpse of these works of the flesh that we can identify in the life of persons being oppressed or possessed by the devil.

Listed below are some of the cohorts of this strongman or general:

FEAR-PHOBIAS: Intense, abnormal illogical fear (see Isaiah 13:7-8, 2 Timothy 1:7 and 1 John 4:18)

TORMENT-HORROR: Great pain or anguish, harassment, an intense feeling of repugnance, fear, intense dislike (see Psalm 55:4-5 and 1 John 4:18)[15]

FEAR OF DEATH: A state of dread (see Psalm 55:4 and Hebrews 2:14-15)

UNTRUSTING-DOUBT: Inability to trust anyone, skeptical (see Matthew 8:26 and Revelation 21:8)

NIGHTMARES-TERRORS: An extremely frightening dream, event, or experience; causing intense distress or intense overpowering fear (see Psalm 91:5-6)

FEAR OF MAN: The total inability to trust men because of fear of death or harm from mankind (see Proverbs 29:25, Isaiah 7:2, Jeremiah 1:8 and Ezekiel 2:3-8)

STRESS: An applied force or system of forces that tends to strain the body, mental or emotional pressure (see 1 Peter 5:7)

ANXIETY: A state of uneasiness, worry (see 1 Peter 5:7)

---

15. This spirit overlaps with the spirit of bondage

PERFECTIONISM: The fear that our works are never good enough, seeking approval (see Ephesians 2:8-9)

HEART ATTACKS: Heart distress due to anxiety or stress (see Psalm 55:4, Luke 21: 26, John 14:27 and 14:1)

PTSD (POST-TRAUMATIC STRESS DIS-ORDER): This is a mental health condition that's triggered by a terrifying event—either experiencing it or witnessing it; may include nightmares, vivid flashbacks, intrusive thoughts, intense distress, physical sensations such as pain, nausea, or trembling (see 2 Timothy 1:7, 1 John 4:18 and Psalm 91:5-6)

As you can see, this general is probably the most dominant of the twelve generals or strongmen we will study. This general affects more than people realize. But fear is not given to the Christian. Paul, in 2 Timothy 1:7, wrote:

God has not given us a spirit to fear, but of power and of love and of a sound mind.

Fear comes from the enemy and not from our Father. This thing FEAR is the enemy's version of our FAITH. Fear is the opposite of FAITH. Everything God has in His realm is of goodness; everything the devil has in his realm is of ungodliness. We must remember: the devil is a liar and deceiver. He tries to copy everything God has created.

God has a domain of righteousness, peace, joy, and eternal life in Christ Jesus in Heaven; the devil has a domain of unrest, hatred, and eternal death outside of Jesus Christ in Hell.

In Psalms 11:10 , the Word tells us: *"The fear of the LORD is the beginning of wisdom."* What is this kind of fear? It is a reverence for the awesomeness of God and His holiness and righteousness. It is giving to Him the respect due Him for His grace and mercy shown toward us. Even when we were in our sinful nature, He was willing to die for us.

One type of fear is controlled by the Holy Spirit, and the other is controlled by a demon spirit. They are total opposites. The apostle John said in Revelation 21:8 that the fearful will be cast into the lake which burns with fire, which is the second death. This fear is not of God, and those who operate in this fear SHALL be judged and punished by death.

144

Again, this is the devil's form of faith for the lost world. The definition of Satan's faith (*fear*) is "a feeling of alarm, a state of dread." For example, "My good works are not enough for salvation, and they never will be good enough." The definition of God's faith is *pis-tis,* which is "persuasive, credence, moral convictions of the truthfulness of God, dependence or reliance upon Christ for salvation."

From the manifestations of the cohort of this strongman, we can see how it affects the human body with many undesirable, unnecessary symptoms, which may eventually lead to death. If left unchecked, this person may also be affected by the spirit of bondage. He comes on the scene and sets up house, and now the person is twice as bad off as in the beginning.

With their fears and inability to relax and sleep for fear of dying or of a man attacking them while they sleep, along comes another of the generals—heaviness—with his insomnia. Now the house is getting more and more crowded.

Many times, when this begins to happen, it's like a dead carcass on the highway. It attracts vultures. I believe this was the state of the man from the Gadarenes. What was the answer given to Jesus when He asked, *"What is your name?"* The spirit answered, *"Legion, for we are many"* (Mark 5:9).

What is the meaning of the word *legion*? It was "a unit of measurement for the Roman army." A legion had anywhere from three thousand to six thousand able-bodied men. This man was in an extremely difficult place with so many demons, imps, and other demonic beings in him. No wonder he lived in the caves and cemeteries and cut himself and had strength that no man could chain him!

These demonic spirits also give a man super-human strength. I have witnessed this in deliverance sessions, small men and women having strength far beyond their own physical capabilities, and the voices that came from them were the sounds of a very large male.

So, how do we deal with this strongman?

FIRST: We cover everyone present (including ourselves) with the blood of Jesus for protection and to prevent this general from entering others and causing more troubles. We also ask if the person is a Christian. If not, then lead them in the sinner's prayer, asking God to forgive their sins and asking Jesus to come into their lives as Lord and Savior.

Next, we must get to the root cause of the fear. It may stem from a volatile past with an ex-mate, family member, or childhood experience. Deal with it at the source.

Many children are traumatized by the death of a mother or father, by having been sexually assaulted, or by having witnessed some horrible event that caused them extreme stress and discomfort or trauma.

When I was a child of about ten or eleven, my sisters and I were in our hometown for an event prior to Thanksgiving. There was a clothing store owner who had hired a pilot and plane to circle over the town and throw out guinea fowl. Anyone who was fortunate enough to catch one of these birds could then take it to the local supermarket and redeem it for a turkey or ham for their Thanksgiving dinner.

As the pilot was making an inside loop to throw out more birds, he failed to estimate his speed and altitude correctly, and therefore nose-dived into the earth just behind a local church, killing both him and the local businessman. It is childhood events such as this that cause fear in the hearts of many people. I'm sure there were many who made inner vows that they would never fly in a plane. We need to get to the root of the fear and deal with it from the root.

SECOND: We bind this strongman and his cohorts and command them to leave the person and return to their place in the pit and never return to them again, according to Mark 9:25. The person has been severely traumatized from this demon and needs intensive ministry. There have been many cases where the ministering went on for weeks (or months) after the initial deliverance session. We, as God's ministers, cannot throw these individuals back to the wolves or, in this case, back to the demonic world to be devoured again.

If it is necessary, continue to talk to them and encourage them. Continue to text them or email them and give them hope and the Word of God. Social media is a wonderful way to minister in these cases because it is instant communication with the person, and these reach around the globe. This activity is supported by Matthew 18:18, 2 Timothy 1:7, Revelation 21:10-27, 22:1-3 and 10:14.

Encourage, encourage, and encourage them some more. By doing so, they become accountable to you before God for their actions. Again, encourage, encourage, and encourage some more.

THIRD: We loose the Holy Spirit with the Spirit of love, power and a sound mind to them (see 2 Timothy 1:7). This will be a new experience for them, to be walking in the peace of God for the first time, probably in many years. The Word tells us:

You SHALL know the truth, and the truth SHALL set you free.   John 8:32
(Emphasis Mine)

How will you recognize this spirit? Matthew 7:20 says, *"By their fruits you [shall} know them."* Watch how they are acting and what they are saying. Out of the abundance of the heart, the mouth speaks. What is in the heart of the individual will come out of their mouth—righteousness or unrighteousness (see Luke 6:45).

Many times I have smelled the demon involved in the person's life. Some have the smell of a sick stomach; some have the smell of smoke or fire from Hell. Have all of your senses operating and discern what is happening.

Exercise your God-given authority and the right to use the name of Jesus Christ to defeat these generals. What is the definition of authority?

"Delegated power, the right to command, to enforce obedience, to make final decisions regarding the devils activity in your life, that of your family, church, and world."

— FOR YOUR NOTES—

CHAPTER 11

SPIRIT OF INFIRMITY

DEFINITION: *"Physical weakness or afflic-tion of the body, usually the five main senses, and the main motor functions of the body, skeletal, muscular, nervous, respiratory, circu-latory, auditory, and sight* (see James 5:13)."

NOTE: The works of the flesh cannot be bound. They are free-will acts of the person, but they are controlled by de-monic spirits that can and must be bound in order to set the person free. Again, Galatians 5:19-21 gives us a glimpse of these works of the flesh that we can identify in the life of persons being oppressed or possessed by the devil.

Listed below are some of the cohorts of this strong-man or general:

BLINDNESS: Inability to see or perceive light (see Mark 8:22 and John 9:1)

LAMENESS: Crippled, especially in a leg, foot, impairing one's ability to walk, such as with MS, MD, etc. (see Leviticus 21:18, Matthew 15:31, 21:14, Acts 3:2, 8:7 and 14:8)

DUMBNESS/MUTE: Inability to speak or make sounds (see Mark 7:32 and 9:25)

AUTISM, SCHIZOPHRENIA: Abnormal subjectivity, any of a group of psychotic reactions caused by demonic influence, mental disorders, (see Matthew 8:28-34 and Mark 5:1-20)

DEFORMITIES: A bodily malformation, such as a club foot, humpback, withered hand, crossed eyes etc. (see Matthew 12:9-14 and Luke 13:10-13)

DEAFNESS: Inability to hear sounds (see Mark 7:31-37, especially verse 32 and 9:25)

These are just a small sample of the works of this general or strongman in and on the human body. This demon is a coward. It attacks the vulnerable baby in the womb of the mother or as it is being birthed from the womb.

As we know, Satan is a thief, a liar, and a murderer. He has been from the beginning, and his tactics have not changed since the beginning of time. He takes every opportunity to destroy God's most prized creation—man.

Satan hates God so much because he was thrown out of Heaven and lost his position as the third archangel. Yes, he was one of just three: Michael, the warring and protector angel, Gabriel, the messaging and information angel, and Lucifer, the angel in charge of praise and worship before the throne of God. But, because of his pride and ambition and his beautiful body and countenance, he said, *"I will exalt my throne above the stars of God"* (Isaiah 14:13). He wanted to receive praise for himself. This was when the battle started in Heaven. Michael and his third of the angelic beings defeated Lucifer and his third of the angelic beings, casting them out of Heaven down to the Earth.

Because we were created in the image and after the likeness of God, we are the "spitting image" of God, and Satan hates us for that. Every time he looks at us, he is reminded of what he once had as an archangel, and it infuriates him. He sees in us his archenemy, Jesus Christ, and tries his best to destroy us.

This is why he takes the opportunity to try to destroy an unborn child in its mother's womb or birth canal. He hates us with a hatred we cannot comprehend. His hatred for us is the total opposite of the love our Father has for us, which is a love we cannot comprehend with our human minds. This is the reason Jesus came to this ungodly Earth and submitted to a brutal death on a wooden cross, to redeem or purchase us back from our ultimate destination—death in Hell.

Remember the prophet Hosea and his marriage to his prostitute wife, Gomer? This union was a symbolic example of the marriage of Jesus to His Bride. Just as Hosea was willing to pay the price for Gomer's redemption, Jesus willing paid the price for His Bride, the Church.

This evil spirit usually attacks during a pregnancy or during the delivery of the baby. It can come from family bloodline curses that have been handed down from Satan and never dealt with in past generations (see Exodus 34:7). It can come from the mother's use of illegal (and even sometimes legal) drugs that affect the child during the gestation period. In any event, all of this comes from our enemy, Satan, and his hatred for the human race.

Many will say, "This came from God to keep us humble." This is a lie from the devil. My Bible says in John 10:10:

The thief does not come except to steal, and to kill, and to destroy. I have come that they may have life, and that they may have it more abundantly.

If any man or demon tries to contradict or change the Word, they are a liar. This is why I add these scriptures to these statements, so that you can prove for yourselves what I and the Word and the Holy Ghost are saying is true. I don't want you to take my word for it just because I have a Ph.D. behind my name. Prove the teachings for yourself.

I have taught these principles for more than thirty years, been in the ministry of deliverance for more than forty years and have seen these teachings work. God backs up His Word. He stands behind those who are truly called into this ministry.

Why did I say, "Truly called into this ministry?" Because there are many who have not been called, but have seen the ministry as a very lucrative business, a way to extract money from unsuspecting and hurting people. They may get away with this for a season, but ultimately they will be dealt with by the Holy Spirit and will pay dearly for their deceptions.

Janice and I never charge anyone for ministering to people in this manner, whether it be counselling or deliverance. This is a gift from the Holy Spirit to us all, and we are merely the vessel He uses.

In 2007, Janice and I were in South Africa in the village of Maphophe ministering. We ministered on these concepts briefly while we were there. After we returned home, Senior Pastor Simon Shirinda called us on the phone and said there was a woman who was pregnant and had never felt the baby move in her body.

The doctor at a nearby clinic did a sonogram on the woman and found that the baby had no head. We prayed and bound this spirit of infirmity, commanded him to release the woman and her unborn baby, and commanded the baby to have a head. Pastor Shirinda called again and said, "Now the baby has a head, but it's too large for the baby to be born naturally. The doctor wants to do a C-section." But as a nurse was wheeling the mother into surgery on the gurney, the baby was born naturally with a head full of beautiful hair.

Later, we saw this baby and mother, and the child was a perfectly formed, healthy baby girl whose name was Pearl. She was named appropriately. Why? Because the mother paid a high price for her baby girl. To God be the glory! This and so many other outstanding miracles were done because: 1) The people believed for their healing or deliverance, and 2) God backed up His Word and proved Himself stronger that the devil.

Some years ago, Janice and I were in a church in South Louisiana, ministering and giving the congregation an update on what the ministry had done with the funds they had provided us to go on trips. As we were telling them of the mighty move of the Holy Spirit and the miracles we were experiencing, a gentleman raised his hand and asked, "Why are you seeing so many miracles in South Africa, and we don't see them here in America?" The Holy Spirit immediately spoke to me and said, "Because the churches in America are inoculated with just enough religion, and it makes them immune to the full power of the Gospel."

How true this statement is. We do see miracles in America, but not on a regular basis. Janice and I have seen the dead raised back to life, blind eyes opened, deaf ears unstopped, barren women give birth to children, broken ribs and punctured lungs healed, and so many others. Why do we see these things happen? Because our Father called us into this ministry in 1979 and mandated us to take it to the sick, possessed, oppressed, and dying world. We have been obedient to that mandate and calling and have studied to show ourselves approved by God.

We're not special people. We're no different than many of you, with one exception. We love our God and trust Him explicitly. I am by no means implying that you don't love and trust God. But it's so important in the deliverance ministry to put all of your trust in God.

We trust that God has given the person being delivered the revelation that they need deliverance. We must also trust that the timing is right and that we are using the discernment of the Holy Spirit. If we doubt that God is in control, we will be going through the motions in the flesh and could become like the seven sons of Sceva. If God called us to do it, then He is obligated to perform whatever is needed to be done, not us. We're merely the vessel He operates through.

So, how do we deal with this strongman or demon?

FIRST: We cover everyone present (including ourselves) with the blood of Jesus Christ for protection and to prevent this unclean spirit from entering

158

anyone else. I have been in meetings where a minister would start deliverance on someone and never cover those present with the blood. The outcome of that meeting was devastating, to say the least. They would also begin to bind the spirits of tobacco, witchcraft, alcohol, adultery, or some other outward manifestation of the true strongman that was controlling them. I could hear that demon just standing there laughing at them for their lack of understanding of the spirit world.

Remember, you, as a true believer in Christ Jesus, have the authority over all of the works of the devil, according to Luke 10:19. Not just some of, part of, or selected groups of his works, but every work of the devil.

I can hear someone who is reading this say in their spirit or even out loud, "He'd better not say that because the devil will hear him say it and come after him." Brothers and Sisters, we are already known in Hell for standing up against the devil and taking back what belongs to our Father. I have heard demons say, "Oh, no, here he comes again." I have also heard in the Spirit, as I was doing deliverance and spiritual warfare, my voice of authority echoing in Hell, as those demons were bound and were setting the person free.

Why was my voice echoing into Hell? Because Satan and his demonic hosts of fallen angels needed to hear the authority of our God being exercised over them, cancelling their assignment against that person.

I want to remind you to find out if the person is a Christian. If not, lead them in the sinner's prayer, asking God for forgiveness of their sins and asking Jesus to come into their lives and be their Lord and Savior.

SECOND: We bind this strongman in the name of Jesus and command him and his cohorts back to the pit they came from and to never return to this person again, according to Mark 9:25. We follow the principles given us in Matthew 16:19 and 18:18 when dealing with these unclean spirits:

Whatever you bind on earth [shall] be bound in heaven, and whatever you loose on earth [shall] be loosed in heaven.

Again, there is that little, seemingly insignificant word *SHALL.* This word has been changed in so many translations of the Bible from *shall* to *will*, but there's a great difference. The word *will* means "with intent, but possibly changed." The word *shall* means "mandatory obligation to be fulfilled or completed." *Will* can be amended; *shall* cannot be amended. It must be completed as ordered.

Why did I refer to the heavenlies instead of Heaven? The original translation stated it that way. There are three levels of Heaven. The first level is the atmosphere that touches the earth. The second is the area of outer space where these unclean spirits operate, and we bind them from entering the first heavenly realm, Earth. The third Heaven is the realm where God lives, which the apostle John referred to (see Revelation 1:8-9) and Paul referred to (see 2 Corinthians 12:2-5). The unclean spirits have no access to this realm (see Luke 10:18).

THIRD: After we are confident of the person's salvation, we loose the Holy Spirit with healing to the person involved. We see this in Matthew 10:1, Mark 6:7 and 13, Acts 10:38, and Isaiah 53:5. Trust the move of the Holy Spirit in you, and listen to His instructions on how to pray and what to pray over the person. He will never steer you wrong. Believe me, we've been doing this for more than forty years, and He has never failed us in any way or at any point.

Again, how will you recognize this spirit? Matthew 7:20 says, *"By their fruits you [shall] know them."* Watch how they are acting and what they are saying. Out of the abundance of the heart, the mouth speaks. What is in the heart of the individual will come out of their mouth—righteousness or unrighteousness (see Luke 6:45).

Many times I have smelled the demon involved in the person's life. Some have the smell of a sick stomach; some have the smell of smoke or fire from Hell, and other such smells. Have all of your senses operating, discerning what is happening, and don't be afraid of the sights that you may see or hear from people as they are being delivered from this strong-man of infirmity. Sometimes Satan can be comical in his exit from people, as you will discover.

Exercise your God-given authority and the right to use the name of Jesus Christ to defeat these generals. What is the definition of authority?

"Delegated power, the right to command, to enforce obedience, to make final decisions regarding the devils activity in your life, that of your family, church and world."

— FOR YOUR NOTES —

— For Your Notes—

CHAPTER 12

SPIRIT OF SICKNESS

DEFINITION: *"Sickness that affects the physical body, brought on by exposure to disease carrying germs, poor diet, hygiene, or exposure to viral or bacterial diseases."*

NOTE: The works of the flesh cannot be bound. They are free-will acts of the person, but they are controlled by demonic spirits that can and must be bound in order to set the person free. Again, Galatians 5:19-21 gives us a glimpse of these works of the flesh that we can identify in the life of persons being oppressed or possessed by the devil.

Listed below are some of the cohorts of this strongman or general, the physical manifestations of this unclean spirit:

BOILS: A painful, pus-filled swelling of the skin (see Deuteronomy 28:35, Job 2:7 and Revelation 16:2)

FEVER-AGUE: An unusually high body temperature brought on by an infection or disease (see Deuteronomy 28:22, Job 30:30, John 4:46-52, especially verse 52 and Acts 28:8)

CANCERS: Any of a variety of malignant neoplasms that manifest invasiveness and have a tendency to metastasize (attach) to new sites, cells, tissues, and grow uncontrollably (see Acts 12:20-24, especially verse 23)

DYSENTERY: An infection of the lower intestine accompanied by fever and severe diarrhea (see Acts 28:8)

CONSUMPTION: The act of being consumed or eaten alive, flesh-eating virus, tuberculosis (see Deuteronomy 28:22)

DROPSY: The accumulation of diluted fluids in the body cavity and tissues, congestive heart failure (see Luke 14:2)

INSANITY: Persistent mental disorders (see Daniel 4:33, Matthew 4:24 and 17:15)[16]

TUMORS-HEMORRHOIDS: A noninflammatory growth arising from existing tissue but growing independently of the normal tissue, itching and painful mass of dilated veins in swollen anal tissues (see Deuteronomy 28:27 and 1 Samuel 5:6)

LOSS OF APPETITE: The loss of the desire to eat food or drink (see Psalm 102:4 and 107:18)

LEPROSY: A chronic, infectious, granulomatous disease ranging in severity from noncontagious to contagious (see Deuteronomy 24:8, Matthew 4:24 and Mark 1:40-43)[17]

Jesus was beaten with a whip called the "cat of nine tails." It was a relatively short whip with nine individual tentacles coming from the handle. Each of these tentacles were imbedded with pieces of glass, bone, or metal, designed to literally rip the skin and flesh from the body of the person being beaten. It was Jewish law that no person could be beaten

---

16. This strongman is also overlapped with the spirit of infirmity
17. There are many more examples of this general, but for the sake of time and space, they are not listed here.

more than "forty times, save one" or thirty-nine. So, Jesus received thirty-nine individual lashes or strikes from this whip. Thirty-nine lashes times nine for the tentacles equals three hundred and fifty-one stripes on His body, not including the incisions and bruises from the imbedded objects in those tentacles. He was marred more than any other man, and theologians say that those lashes and puncture wounds were for the healing of EVERY disease known to man on this earth—then and now.

This general attacks the physical body with many symptoms, from fever to nausea, vomiting, shakes, cancers, measles, mumps, childhood sicknesses, TB, blood disorders, etc. (see James 5:14).

The Word of God tells us that there is nothing new under the sun (see Ecclesiastes 1:9). What Jesus dealt with in His day is the same things we are dealing with today. Satan has not changed his tactics for trying to maim and kill us. The only difference today is the existence of social media, reaching nearly every person on planet Earth, plus more doctors and better medicines.

But there are still some sicknesses or diseases that medicine cannot cure. In fact, the overuse of some medications, such as antibiotics, it is causing serious problems in the medical field. Some sicknesses have become drug resistant and no longer respond to the medications designed to kill the viruses causing them.

The apostle James, the half-brother of Jesus, said in James 5:14-15:

> *Is anyone among you sick? Let him call for the elders of the church, and let them pray over him, anointing him with oil in the name of the Lord. And the prayer of faith will save the sick, and the Lord will raise him up. And if he has committed sins, he will be forgiven.*

This is in the Word of God used in every Bible-believing church, yet there are "preachers" not following the formula for God's ordained healing process. Instead, they have bought into the lie from the devil that healing and deliverance passed away with the early disciples. WELL, PRAISE GOD, they're wrong. Healing and deliverance are still available today.

Every person who professes Jesus as their Lord and Savior, allows Him to lead and guide them, and studies to further their understanding of the King of Kings, is a disciple of Jesus Christ. God's Word is for each of them. This lie, that healing and deliverance are no longer available, was passed down by some demon-controlled official in some denominational office that has been lied to by Satan. Don't believe it!

As a child growing up in the early 1940s and 50s in a small rural Baptist Church here in Central Louisiana, there was the Creed of the Southern Baptist denomination attached to the door of our baptistery. I would stop and read that creed as a child and tried to commit it to memory. It said:

SALVATION IN JESUS' NAME ONLY, WATER BAPTISM FOR THE REMISSION OF SINS, THE INFILLING OF THE HOLY GHOST WITH THE EVIDENCE OF SPEAKING IN OTHER TONGUES, ANOINTING THE SICK WITH OIL IN THE NAME OF JESUS FOR THE HEALING OF THE SAINTS, THE RAPTURE OF THE CHURCH, AND THE SECOND COMING OF JESUS, AND ...

There was more that I can't remember after seventy years. Sadly, this creed was removed by some big shot preacher or church official out of the national headquarters. As a result, how many people were denied the awesome experience of having God heal them of their sicknesses? What will these big shots say when they stand before a holy, righteous God and be required to give account for their actions?

Will they hear the Judge tell them, "Depart from Me, you worker of iniquity, into everlasting damnation, for I never knew you?"

That creed in that little Baptist church is what started me searching for the truth about healing and praying for sick people at the age of eight or nine. As I noted, I was saved and filled with the Holy Ghost with the evidence of speaking in other tongues in that little church at six years old. It happened on February 18, 1951. It was such an awesome experience that I fell in love with Jesus, and seventy-one years later, I'm still in love with Him.

Not long ago my grandson related to me that his wife found a large lump in her left breast. I prayed for her and cursed the cancer in the name of Jesus. Later, I asked what the biopsy had revealed. He said the doctor couldn't find anything. The lump was gone. This is part of my exercising my God-given authority to bind this strongman and command him to return back to his place in the pit he came from and never return to her again.

I know personally that this works. In 1980, I suffered from prostate cancer. The pain was so severe I couldn't sleep at night. Early one morning I was awakened by severe pain and got out of bed to go to the bathroom to try to get some relief. As I turned to go to the bathroom, there, standing at the foot of my bed, were two beings. As I stepped to the foot of the bed, the closer being reached His hand out and touched me in my groin area. I saw in His hand the hole from the nail that had held Him to the cross. When He touched me, it was as though someone had stuck my fingers in a 230 volt AC electrical socket. At the same instant, it was as though someone had ripped the roof off of my house and filled it with millions of bouquets of flowers that I had never smelled before. IT WAS GLORIOUS![18]

I stumbled on into the bathroom and just sat down on the commode, totally drunk in the Spirit of God. As I sat there, trying to get my composure back and to understand what had just happened, I heard Jesus tell me that He had healed me of the cancer and that He was calling me to pray for people who were afflicted by this disease.

He said to me, "You are to pray for them and curse the root of the cancer as I cursed the root of the fig tree (see Mark 11:12-25). The cancer shall die from the root and shrivel up and leave, and the person shall be healed."

Over the past forty plus years I have been obedient to the instructions of Jesus and have seen Him

---

18. My guess is that the other heavenly being I saw that night was an angel.

perform what He promised to do—heal the sick. It was later that I learned the fragrance of the flowers was the anointing oil and embalming spices they anointed Jesus' body with for His burial.

My wife, Janice, was an Oncology RN at a major hospital, and she would do the same thing as well. She would place a scripture note on the bed or wall of as sick patient with Ezekiel 16:6 and have them pray that scripture over themselves daily. She, too, saw the power of the Lord Jesus in operation, and many of those patients who were obedient to follow her instructions were healed and went home. Janice learned this from my experience in Sulphur, Louisiana, the day I was healed from the cancer that Satan had tried to place on me.

Understand one thing: OUR God is stronger and more powerful than ANY situation or circumstance you or I will ever go through in our entire lives. All we are required to do is ask and receive our healing.

So, again, how do we deal with this general?

FIRST: We cover everyone present (including ourselves) with the blood of Jesus for protection to prevent this strongman from entering others and causing even more problems. This strongman, like ALL the rest of these strongmen, is NOT a gentleman, as our Lord and His Holy Spirit are. These evil spirits will take any advantage to inhabit you and destroy you. Why? These are the orders given to them from their master and lord, Satan.

At this point, again, we must find out if the person is a Christian or not. If not, then lead them in the sinner's prayer, asking God for forgiveness of their sins and asking Jesus into their lives to be their Lord and Savior.

SECOND: We anoint them with oil in the name of Jesus according to James 5:14 and pray the prayer of faith over them, and the prayer of faith shall heal them, and if they have committed any sins, they shall be forgiven. Then we bind this strongman in the name of Jesus Christ and command it to leave, and return to the pit it came from (according Matthew 18:18) and to never return again to the person (according to Mark 9:25). Again, we have been given a formula, or recipe, for success in this ministry, and if we follow it, we shall be successful, for it is God's promise that cannot fail.

Someone asked Pastor Kenneth Copeland on one occasion, "What would you do if you prayed for a sick person and they were not healed?" He calmly replied, "I would go on to the next person, because it's not me that's doing the healing; its God."

174

THIRD: Now we loose the Holy Spirit anointing to this person with the covenant of healing, bought and paid for by Jesus Christ with His blood and stripes. As it says in Isaiah 53:5:

> *He was wounded for our transgressions,*
> *He was bruised for our iniquities;*
> *The chastisement of our peace was upon Him,*
> *And by His stripes we are healed.*

This is a package deal. We can't pick and choose what parts of a covenant we accept; it's the whole package or nothing at all.

There are other scriptural references that we can also look to for confirmation (1 Peter 2:24, Mark 6:7 and 13, 16:17-18, and Acts 10:38).

If you have ever wondered what Jesus went through for our healing and salvation, I encourage you to watch the movie "The Passion of the Christ." This is a modern-day rendering of the trial, the brutality of the beatings, and then the crucifixion of Jesus. It shows a snippet or condensed version of what took place. We took a copy of the movie to South Africa in 2009 and presented it to the church members in Maphophe. There were little children with their faces against the walls and on the floor weeping uncontrollable, adults sobbing and many repenting for what they had made Jesus suffer for their sins. As a whole, their comments were, "After seeing that movie, I will never take my salvation for granted or sin again."

Brothers and sisters in Christ Jesus, it's NOT about you and me at all, but about our Lord and Savior, Jesus Christ. It's what He did to rescue us from the snare of the fowler and his demonic forces. This book is a small attempt to help you, my family in Christ Jesus, to be set free from the enemy and help others to do the same.

I dearly love teaching these lessons and seeing the light bulb come on in the spirits of many people who have thought there was no hope. In 2009, as we were teaching these lessons in South Africa, one lady came to us later. She said she had suffered severe pain in her breast for many years and just knew it was cancer. After the teaching that night, she took authority over the sickness and sent it back to Hell, and received her healing. Now she had no more pain and no more cancer.

On another night, after spending the day with the king and asking him to teach us what it meant to be the child of a king, we went to church, and I gave my testimony about being shot through the head. As I gave the invitation for prayer, I told the congregation of fifteen hundred to two thousand that I knew many of them had been praying and asking God to heal and deliver them, but God was neither healing them nor hearing their prayers. Why? Because they had unforgiveness toward someone who had hurt them, physically, financially, sexually, or mentally. Until they forgave those people, they would not be healed or delivered.

I asked them that if they were included in that group to please raise their hands. About six hundred people raised their hands signifying that they were among that number. I then led them in prayer, forgiving those who had hurt them and releasing them to God for Him to deal with, then asking Him to forgive *them* for their bitterness and anger toward those people. Two nights later, one lady came and asked to give her testimony regarding that night. She said, "As I finished the prayer of forgiving and releasing those who had hurt me, it was as if someone placed my fingers in an electric power socket."

She had been suffering with five life-threatening diseases: AIDS, diabetes, TB, uncontrollable high blood pressure, and a bad heart from a heart attack. She had returned to the doctor on Monday, and he had retested her for every symptom. She testified that the AIDS test was negative, the TB test was negative, the diabetes test was normal, the blood pressure was normal, and she had now the heart of a twenty year old. God had totally healed her, because she had forgiven all of those people who had wronged her.

This testimony opened the flood gate, and person after person began to come and give testimony of what God had done in their lives after they, too, had forgiven their attackers or someone who had wronged them. This is what it's all about, setting the captives free. Here is the prayer I led those people in to be free:

Father, I come to you in the name of Jesus Christ. I have sinned against You by having unforgiveness, hatred, and bitterness in my heart against those who have hurt me physically, mentally, financially, sexually, or some other way. Father, I am holding them in the palm of my hands, and I now lift them up to You for You to deal with. I forgive them and turn them over to You, for You to deal with as You see fit.

Now, Father, please forgive *me* for the sin of bitterness, anger, revenge, hatred, and unforgiveness I have had in my heart toward them.

Cleanse me of this sin and help me to carry Your anointing in me and on me.

In Jesus' name,

AMEN!

If you prayed this prayer, thank God for your deliverance and coming healing. He is no respecter of persons. If He did it for one, He will do it for you. Our Father is a faithful GOD, FATHER, and DADDY. He loves us more than we could ever imagine or comprehend. Spend time with Him in His Word, in prayer, and get to know Him as I do, and you will see that I'm right. Keep studying and learning of our Father and His love for you and your family.

Be richly blessed.
Dr. Michael Fluitt

— FOR YOUR NOTES—

CONCLUSION

We are children of the Most High King, the Ruler, the Owner, and the Creator of everything. With His power, His authority, His Word, His blood, and His Holy Spirit, there is nothing that can prevent us from being successful apostles, prophets, evangelists, pastors, and teachers of God's Word.

God has delegated His power and authority to us. He has given us the right to use the name of Jesus, to bind up the devil and all of his works and to enforce God's obedience over the devil. He has given His Word to back us up in every situation when we are confronted by the devil and we make decisions concerning his works in our lives. Our God is King over all creation, and we are part of His family.

Remember the definition of the word *authority:* "power as delegated to another; the right to command; to enforce obedience; and make final decisions regarding the works of the enemy in our lives." Take the Word of God and walk in the power of the Holy Spirit, and be what God has called you to be in this earth—a representative of Heaven in the presence of men. Allow them to see the love of Jesus Christ in you, and walk as Jesus did among them, doing good and healing those who need healing and deliverance, for God is with you.

Remember whose you are and who you are in Christ Jesus. Allow Him to live His life through you and walk in the assurance that *"[you] can do all things through Christ who strengthens [you]"* (Philippians 4:19).

Maranatha!

REFERENCES

My research for this book was done primarily through the following books:

1. *American Heritage Dictionary of the English Language*, published by Houghton Mifflin Harcourt, New York, NY.

2. *The New Strong's Exhaustive Concordance of the Bible*, published by Thomas Nelson Publishers, Nashville, TN.

3. *The Thomas Nelson Chain Reference New King James Version Study Bible*, published by Thomas Nelson Publishers, Nashville, TN.

4. *The Holy Bible, New Living Translation*, published by Tyndale House Publishers, Inc., Carol Stream, IL.

5. *A Divine Revelation of Hell: Time Is Running Out!* by Mary K. Baxter, published by Whitaker House, New Kensington, PA.

— FOR YOUR NOTES—

ABOUT THE AUTHOR

MICHAEL D. FLUITT was born in Jena, Louisiana on July 11, 1945. He was brought up in a Christian home and taught the Word by his mother, Minnie, and Grandmother, Leonie. He was a member of a small Baptist church in Nebo, Louisiana, where, on February 18, 1951, he was saved and filled with the Holy Spirit. In 1959, the Holy Spirit called him into the ministry at the age of fourteen. He began to minister in surrounding towns, preaching in many churches and youth revivals.

In 1959, God also placed on him a burden for the continent of Africa, and he began to pray for the African people. He continued to minister as the doors were opened to him, but his burning desire was to be a missionary to Africa. Over the next forty years, he met many ministers from Africa who were a result of his intercession for that continent.

In 1961, after proving his faithfulness to the call to the ministry of the Lord, he was licensed as a

Minister in the United Baptist Church. He continued to minister and help in every way possible in the church. He was very active in the Royal Ambassadors.

Upon his graduation from Jena High School in 1964, He enrolled in Louisiana College, where he majored in Biblical Studies. He left there after one year to pursue electronics and moved to New Orleans. In 1965, he earned his Associates Degree in Electronics and successfully completed and passed the First Class Federal Communications Commission (FCC) License test and received his License.

From there, he moved to Wichita Falls, Texas, and worked as an engineer in both standard broadcast and telecommunications. It was there that he met his future wife, Janice Kay Smith. They were married in January 1967 and moved to the Lake Charles/Sulphur, Louisiana area where he, again, worked in standard broadcast as chief engineer and announcer for several radio stations.

In 1979, while working as the manager of a two way/microwave shop, he started attending a Full Gospel Church, and he and his wife both became very active in the ministry. He attended Word of Life Bible College, where he obtained his Bachelors Degree in Biblical Studies, with a Masters to follow in 1987. He worked as Associate Pastor and Youth Pastor from 1980 until 1987. During that time, he also was a Louisiana State Level Commander in the Royal Rangers under the Assemblies of God.

In 1988, he moved into his own pastorate, and he and his wife served in a small country church in Starks, Louisiana until 1989, when he moved to Alexandria, Louisiana. There, he was a microwave engineer, and in 1992, went to work for Century Telephone Company, from which he retired as an engineer in 2006. It was during this time that, after more than forty years, God finally opened the door for him to realize his childhood dream of being a missionary to Africa.

In May 2001, he and his wife, Janice, were invited to go on a mission trip to South Africa with a young evangelist from South Africa, Dr. David McDonald. This opened the door for many years of breathtaking experiences and awesome miracles that some ministers only dream of seeing. They returned to South Africa in 2002 to begin to establish churches in a place where no one was ministering: Kruger National Park. They continue to witness the awesomeness of God in miracles, signs, and wonders.

They have established twelve churches in the park and now minister with a young minister, pastor, evangelist, and his minister wife, Pastors Simon and Elizabeth Shirinda, in The Born Again Christian Church, Maphophe, Limpopo Province, Republic of South Africa. They are responsible for more than eighty other churches in the South Africa National Parks System, plus churches in Nigeria and Uganda.

In 2008, he finally obtained his Doctorate in Biblical Studies from Glendale University. Only God knows what is in the future, but you can rest assured it will be filled with the glory of God.

To date, Dr. Michael and Rev. Janice Fluitt have three children, Michael, Jr., Michelle, and Kimberly, thirteen grandchildren, and twenty-one great-grand-children. How many more only God knows, but each is a God-sent blessing to them. All of their children help them in their ministry in one way or another.

He says, "To those of you who believe God has called you to the ministry or some special calling, never give up on what you believe God has called you to do. Remember, it is in His timing, not yours. It took forty years for me to realize my childhood dream. I had to go through the same thing Paul (Saul) went through after his conversion. He was sent to the backside of the desert for three and a half years to be taught by the Holy Spirit the principles of God. I, too, had to be brought to the place where I could believe God and trust His Word to me. I was also taught to do battle in preparation for the ministry of deliverance that He would call us into. It was this portion of the ministry that would be used more than we would ever know.

"Allow God to mold and train you in what He wants, and stop looking at people. After all, it is not people that you must please and answer to, but God, so please Him."